Effective manager series:

DIY Guide in customising Staff Annual Leave Planner & Roster using Google Sheets

A step-by-step pictorial approach

2nd Edition

Singson Kwan

BSc. (Hons), ADMS, SpecDipHP

Invention

Singson Invention

2017

First Printing: 2017

ISBN 978-0-9986199-0-3

Singson Invention

Singapore

Email: singsoninvention@gmail.com

Contents

Preface

Thank you for picking up this guide and allowing me to share my findings with you!

As good people manager, we always aim at achieving a win-win situation - ensuring smooth running of the operational unit as well as meeting staff personal needs in terms of leave taking. Through years of observation, I came to realise leave clashing among staff is one of the key operational problems which creates negative impact on working relationship among team members. A lot of time has been spent on handling and tackling leave related issues which indirectly affects the overall productivity.

I have been studying and searching both intensively and extensively for a cost-effective way to facilitate the handling /management of staff leave projection and allocation. However, most off-the-shelf human resource or roster planning software are usually catered for local computer installation requirement. Most are not fully transparent in the sense that they are designed for manager use instead of providing online shared access for other staff. Lacking in flexibility of customization, ready-made software(s) is also unlikely to suit the actual need of your unit. In addition, the cost of the afore mentioned software(s) could prove to be too exorbitant for a small department in terms of justifying budget planning. All these pre-existent issues and shortcomings have inspired me to find a "solution", thus developing a DIY system to help managers, departmental heads or anyone involved in tackling this managerial challenge became my utmost priority.

In the following chapters, I will walk you through the steps in how to create an online leave planner which can be made accessible by members of your staff. I hope you will find this book purposive, concise and practical in bringing in benefits to you and your team!

Free feel to email me at ***singsoninvention@gmail.com*** if you have any feedbacks, thoughts and ideas regarding this book. Do share with me if you have interest in any form of collaboration in future book or apps co-authoring. My areas of interest include general management and eye care and vision related topics in health promotion, home-design and ergonomics etc.

Developing insights through continuous learning and sharing
Singson Kwan

Introduction

Who is this guide aimed at?

This guide is designed for managers or team-leaders who are assigned to take charge of staff leave planning and approval duties. By integrating information technology and human psychology, this book helps people managers create a shared leave projection platform for advanced leave planning for the team colleagues.

What are the aims of this guide?

This guide aims to provide a cost-effective method to customise a leave planner and roster so that both manager and staff have a high visibility or transparency of leave availability even before and during leave projection stages. The following are the salient features of the planner:

- ✓ Staff can project his leave and makes changes anytime and anywhere using computer or smartphone
- ✓ It shows real-time changes made by other team members simultaneously even while in the process of any editing that might be going on
- ✓ Staff can have a good overview -in terms of the leave availability on different dates
- ✓ Entire staff team are able to view the planner at any given time, however, the editing of the cells and rows feature will be disabled unless given edit permission
- ✓ Manager can review the editing history made by all staff
- ✓ Manager can set up alert to auto-highlight leave clashes
- ✓ Manager can freeze certain portion of the planner once staff projection period ends

How do I use this guide?

This guide is designed to be read and /or implemented in sequential order, failing so, would result in a less than desired outcome. This guide uses pictorial displays and flowchart descriptions to aid the demonstration. Once you have successfully create the sample planner, you can tailor-made a new one for your company or your department. If you would like to have the sample planner used in the guide, you may email me at ***singsoninvention@gmail.com*** after obtaining this book. Just let me know the purchase details and your Gmail address for verification purposes. I will endeavour to respond to you in the quickest time possible.

Chapter 1)

Create shared folder and Sheets file in Goggle Drive

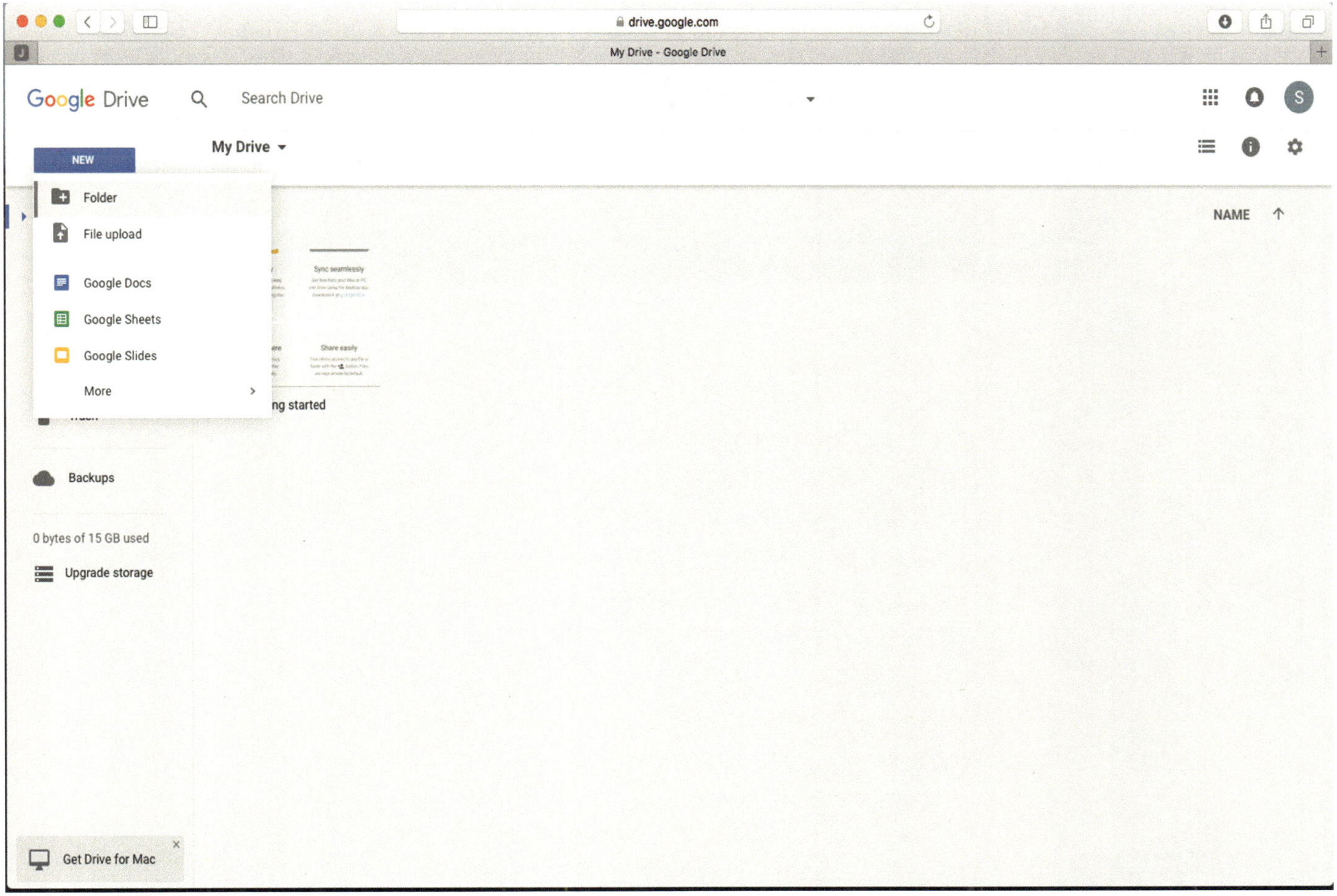

Apply for a Google account and go to Google Drive

Go to google.com to apply for an user account → Log in to the Google account → Go to Google Drive → Left click "NEW" → Left click "Folder"

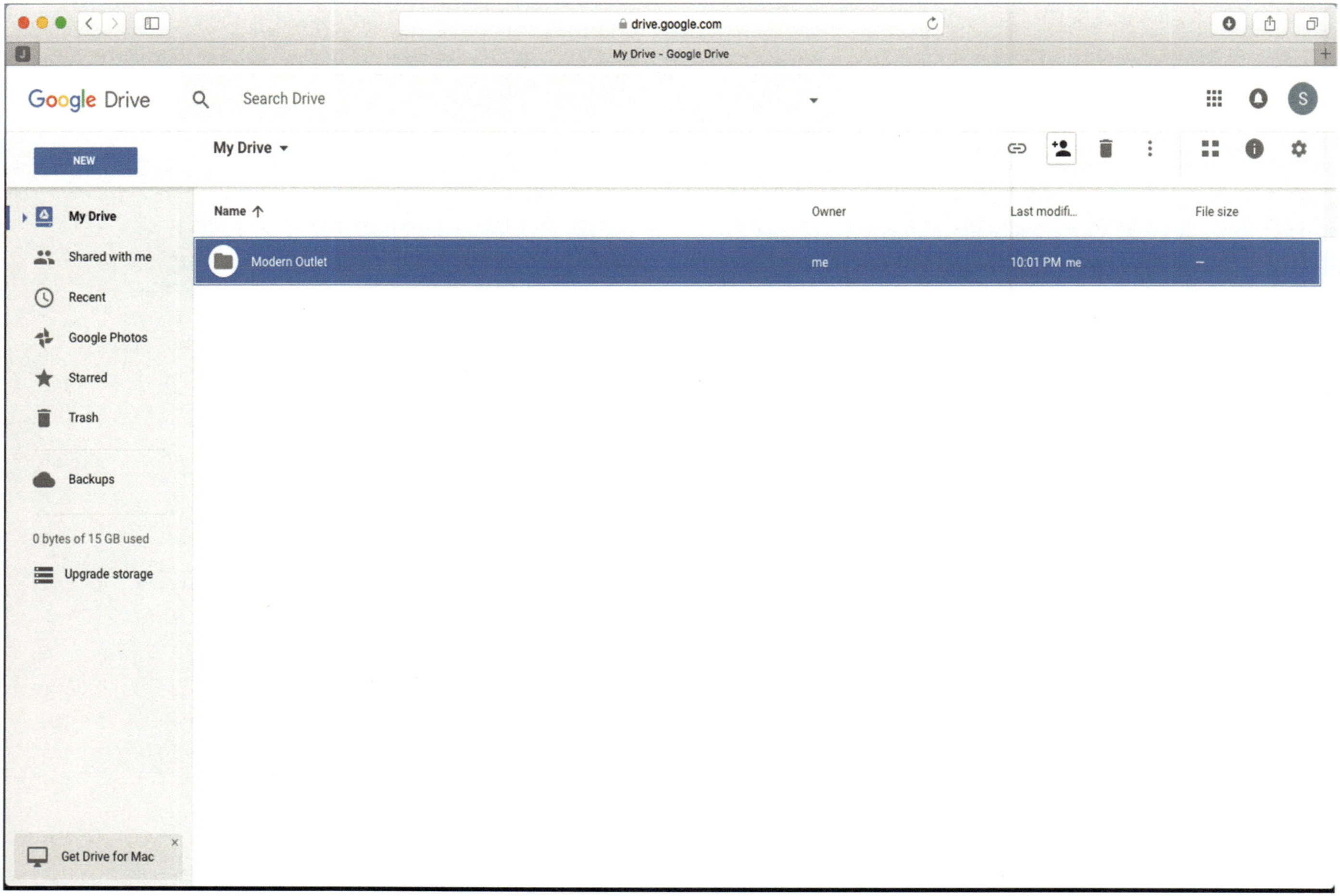

Name the folder using the company name – "Modern Outlet"

Type "Modern Outlet" in pop up window → Press "Create" upon completion

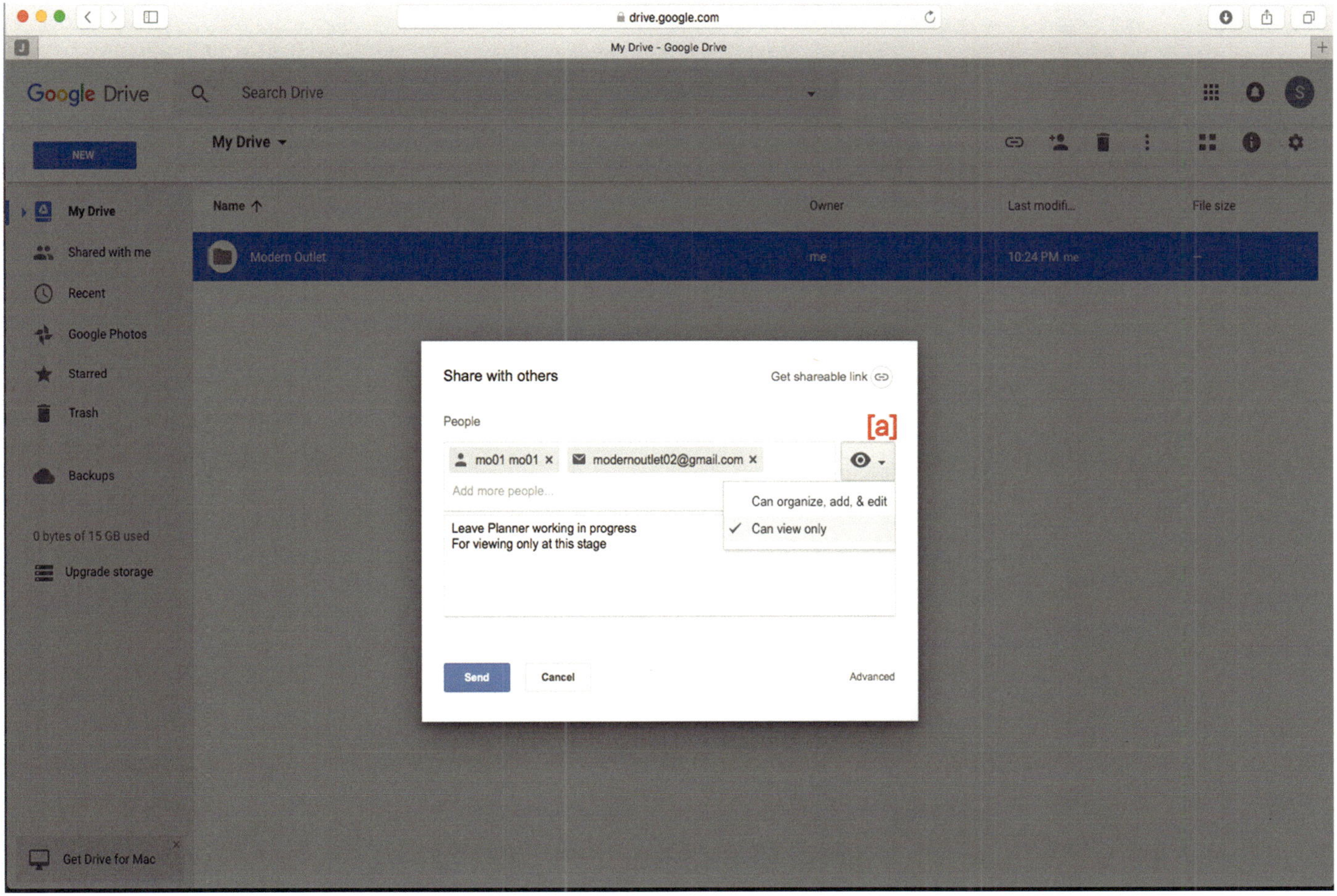

Share the folder with staff who work in Modern Outlet

1. Right click the "Modern Outlet" folder
2. Left click "Share..."
3. Enter the email addresses of all staff
4. Type in the message to be sent out
5. Left click on the icon **[a]**
6. Left click "Can view only"

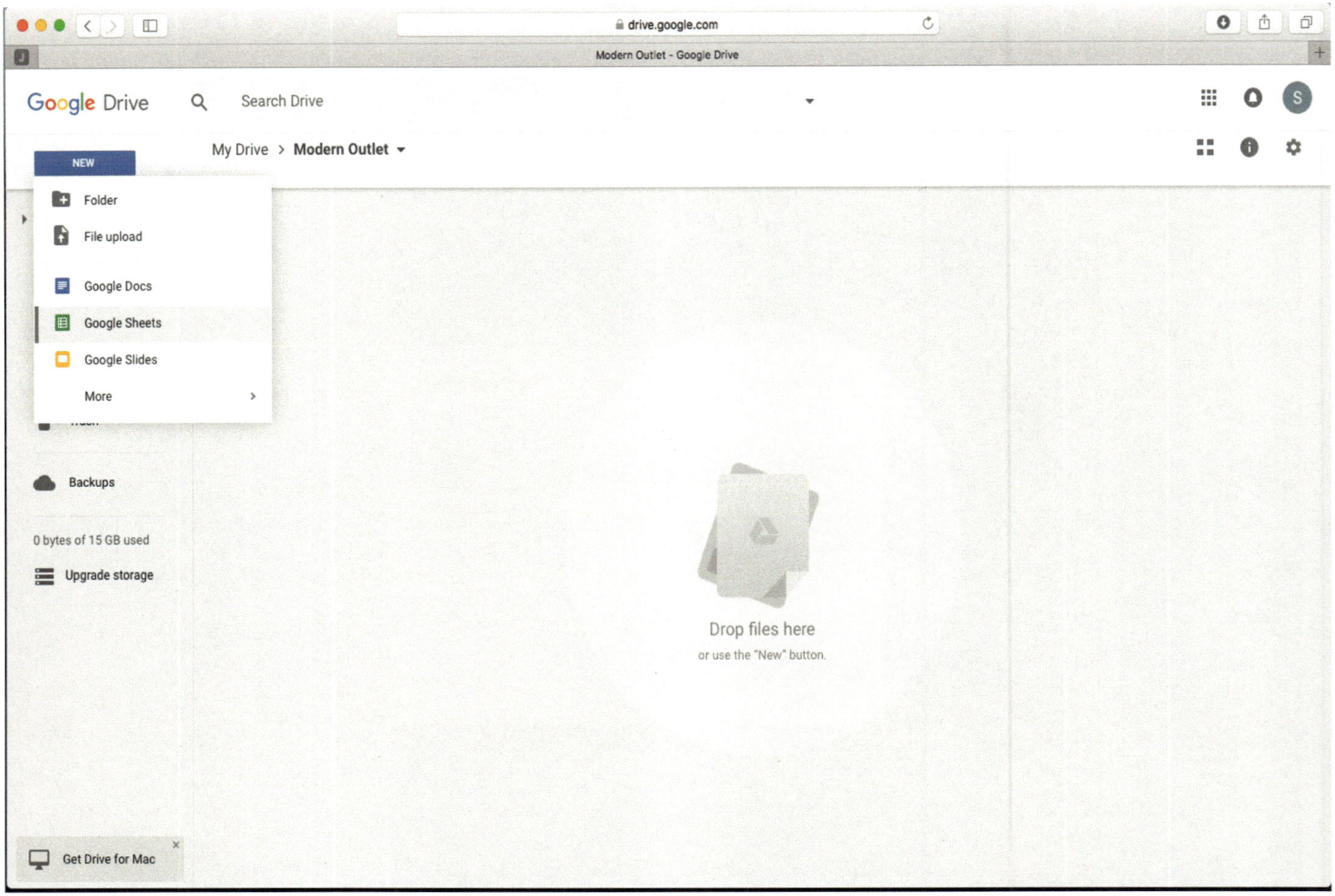

Create a new Google Sheets

Left click "NEW" → Left click "Google Sheets"

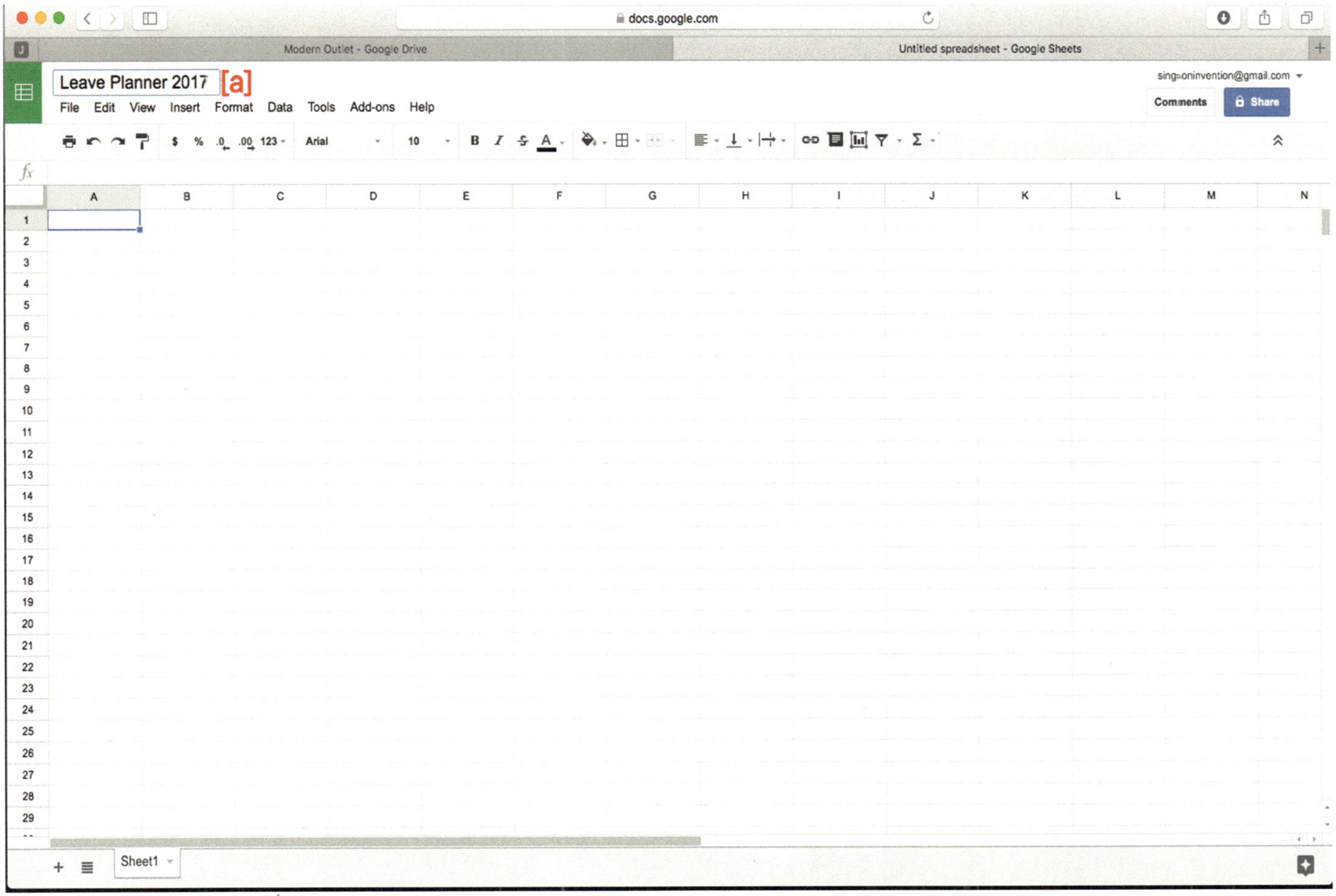

Rename the Google Sheets as "Leave Planner 2017"

1. Left click on [a]
2. Type "Leave Planner 2017"

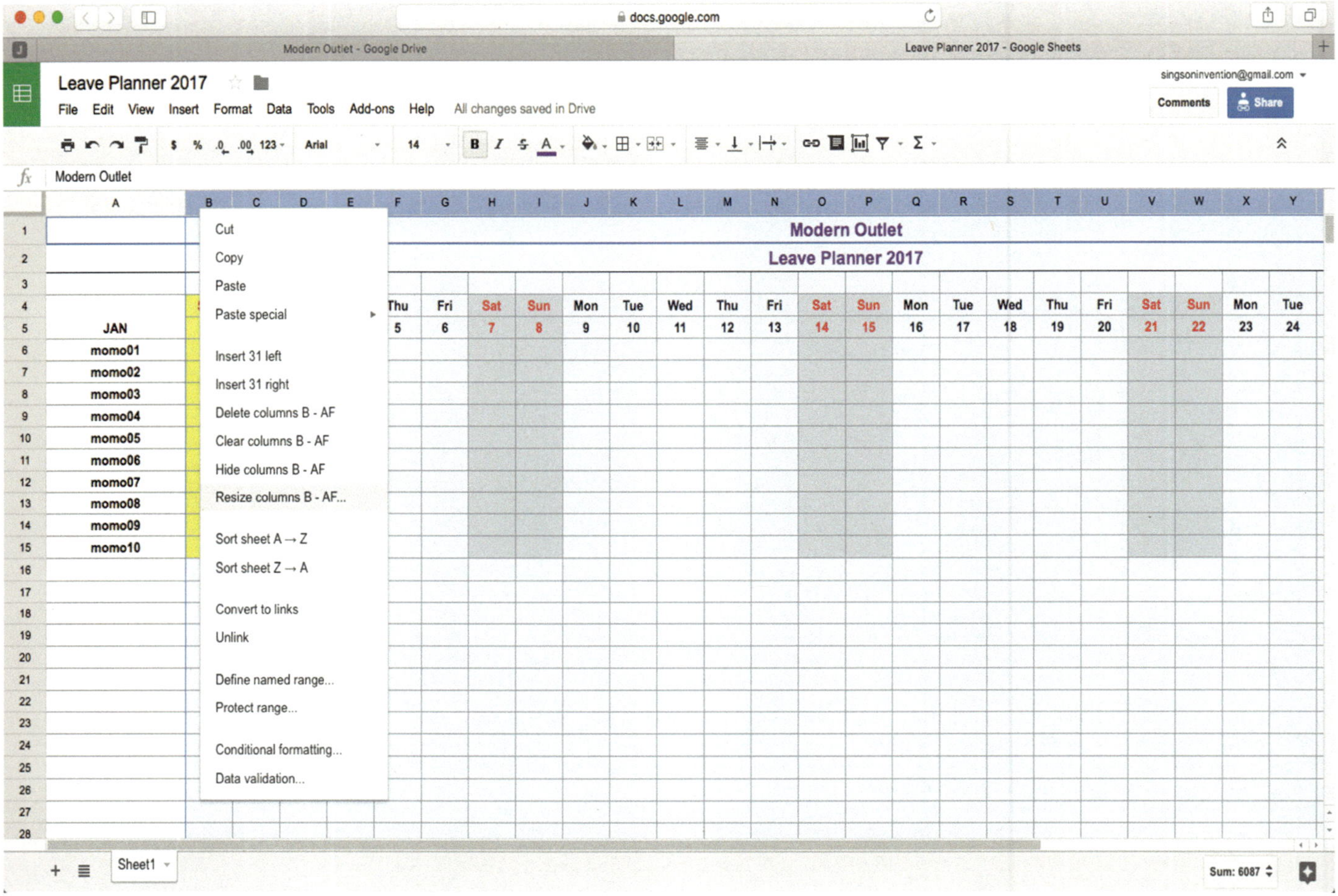

Create the calendar format and type in the staff names and dates for Jan

- Left click and hold to select multiple columns
- Right click to show the menu
- Left click "Resize column..." (e.g. set as 50)
- Type in dates and staff names for Jan (momo01 to momo10)

Chapter 2)

Set up Conditional Formatting Rules

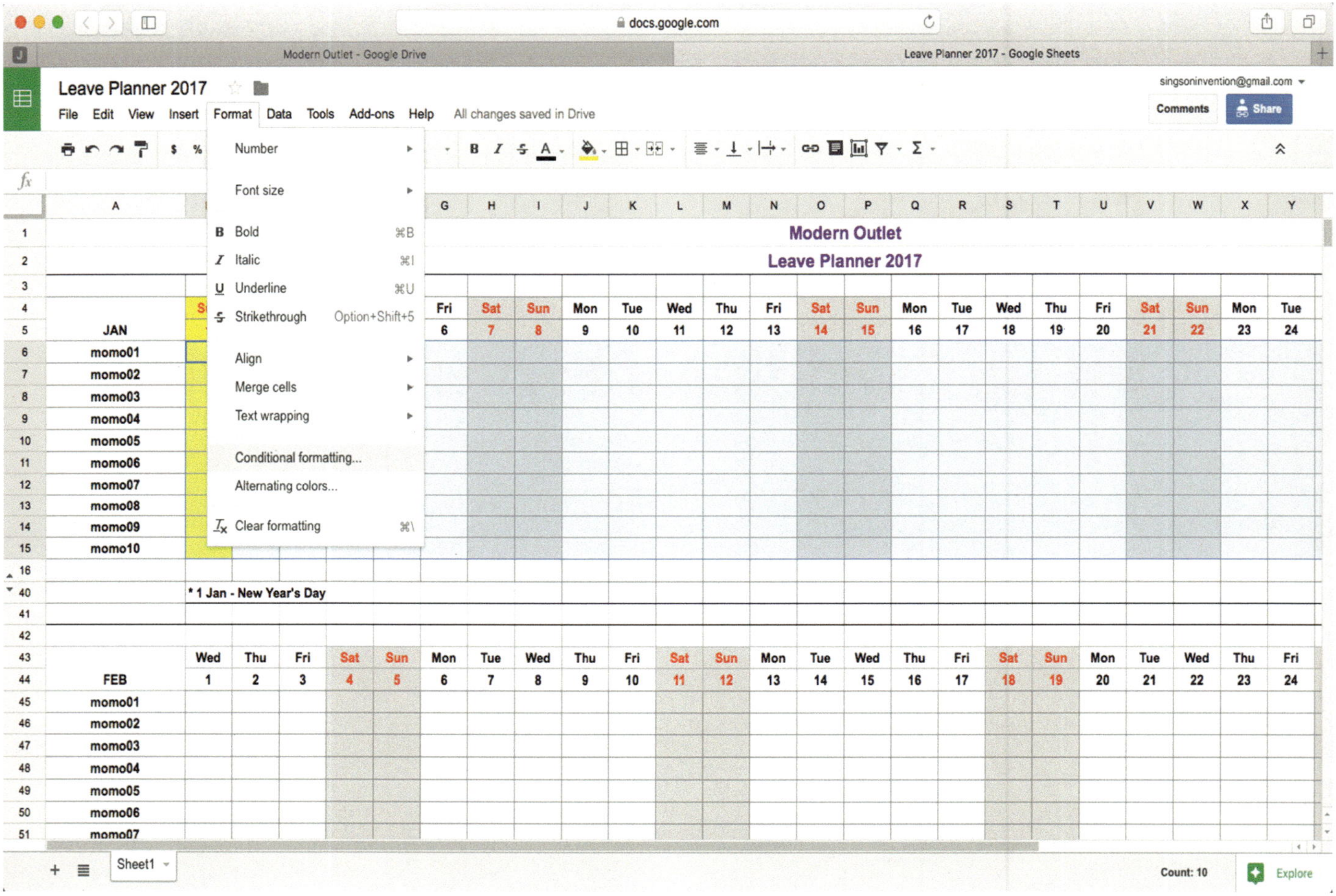

Set up Conditional formatting so that entries hitting certain criteria will be highlighted

1. Left click and hold to select cells that require conditional formatting (i.e.cells B6 to AF15 for 01-31 Jan)
2. Go to toolbar
3. Left click "Format"
4. Left click "Conditional formatting"

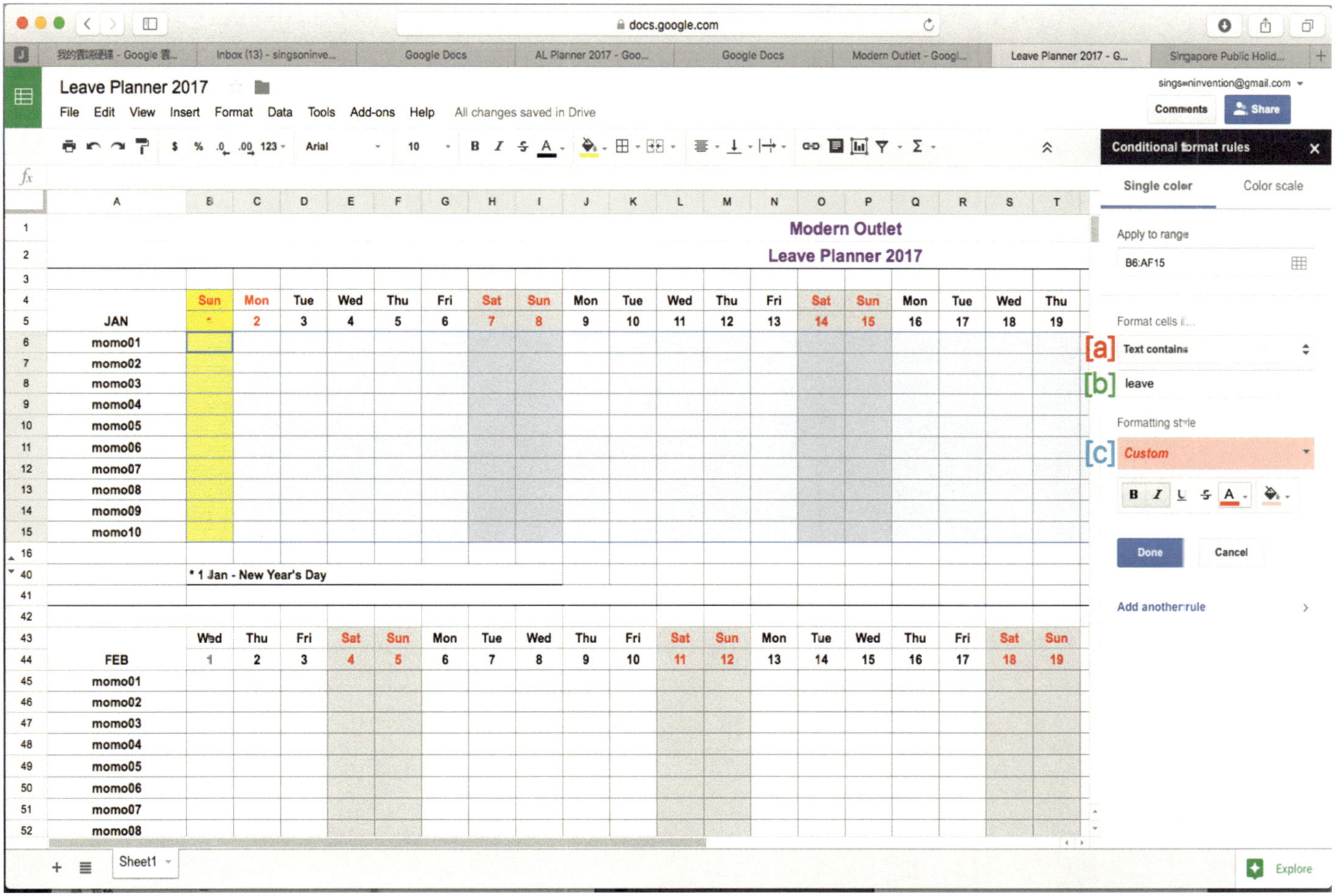

Configure Conditional formatting rules

Left click [a] to choose the condition (e.g. Text contains)

Type in word in that needs to be highlighted in [b] (e.g. “leave”)

Choose the Formatting style in [c] (e.g. words in red, bond, italic and background in pink)

Press “Done” upon completion

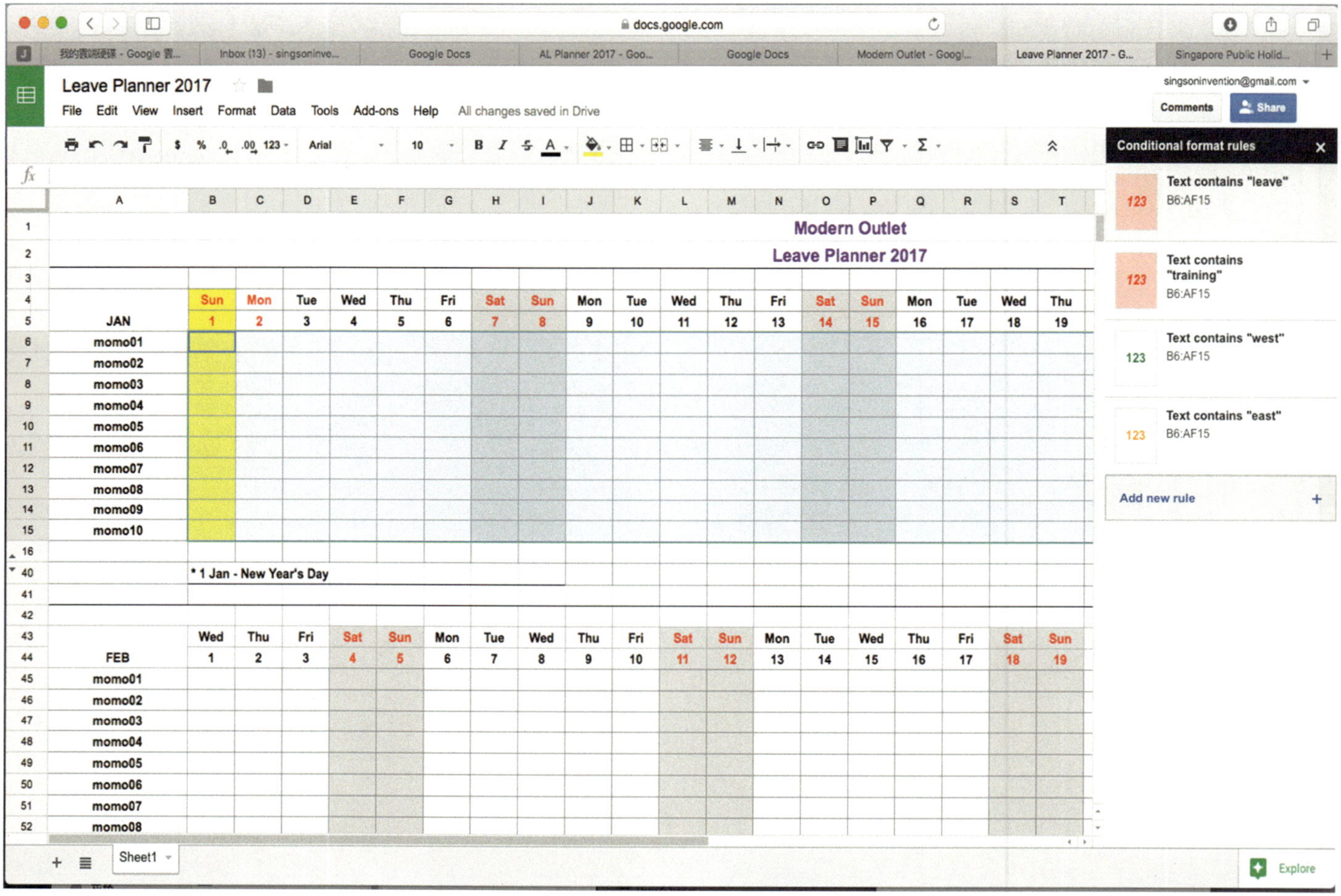

Add new rule(s)

1. After configuring the 1st rule
2. Left click "Add another rule"
3. Repeat the steps in the previous slide
4. Create rules for texts contains "leave", "training", "west" and "east"

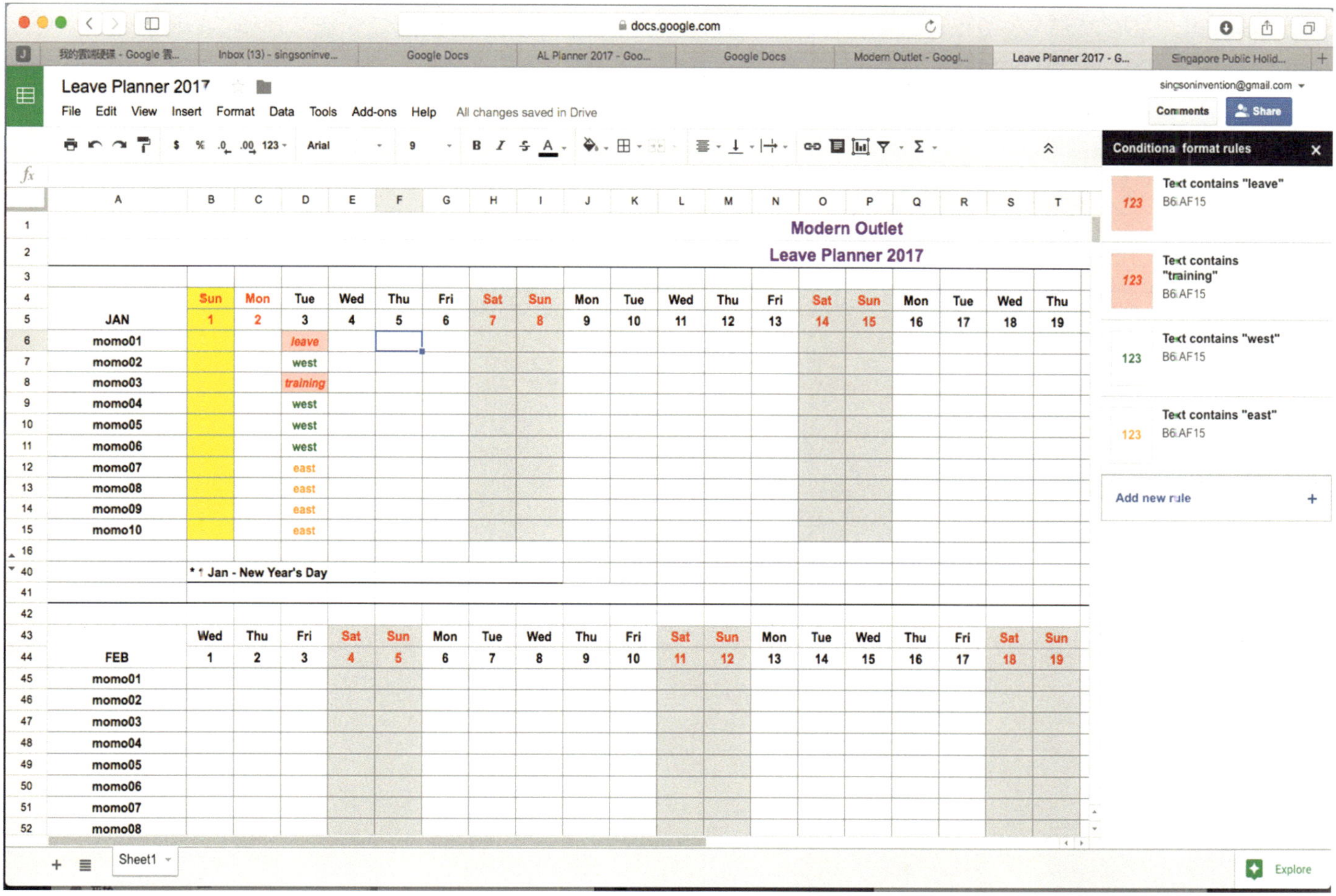

 # Assuming Modern Outlet has two branches –one in the East district and one in the West district

Test the Conditional formatting setup

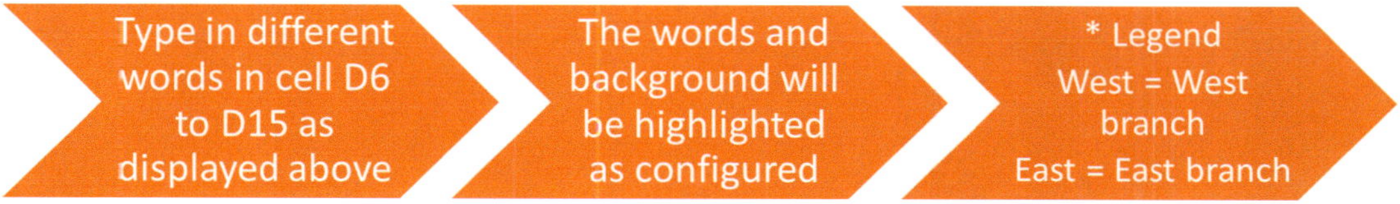

Chapter 3)

Set up of Clashing Alert

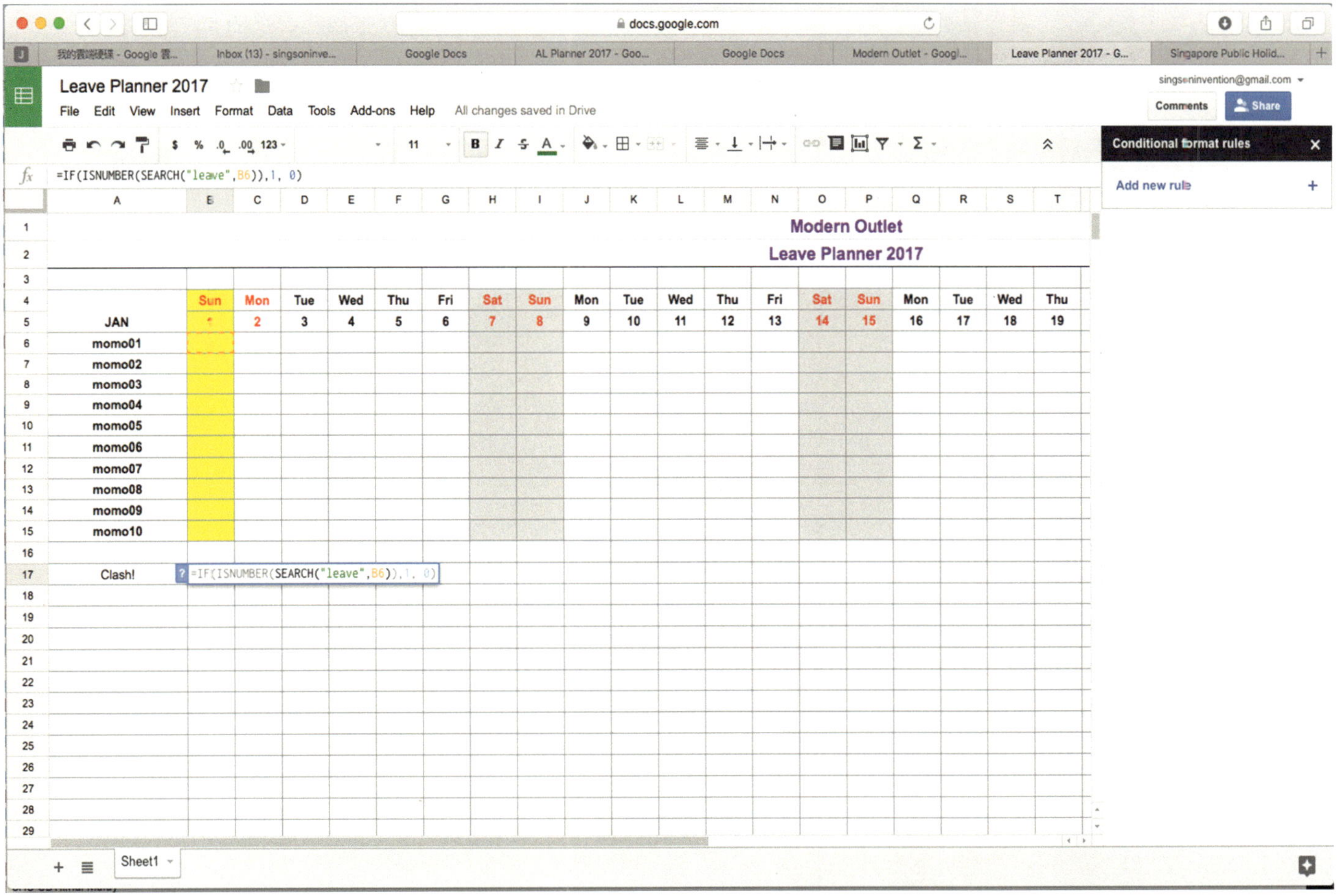

Set up auto-counting function of "leave" for staff momo01 on 01-Jan

1. Set up auto-count for "leave" for momo01 for 01-Jan
2. Left double click on cell B17
3. Type in formula **=IF(ISNUMBER (SEARCH("leave", B6)),1,0)**
4. Press Enter upon completion

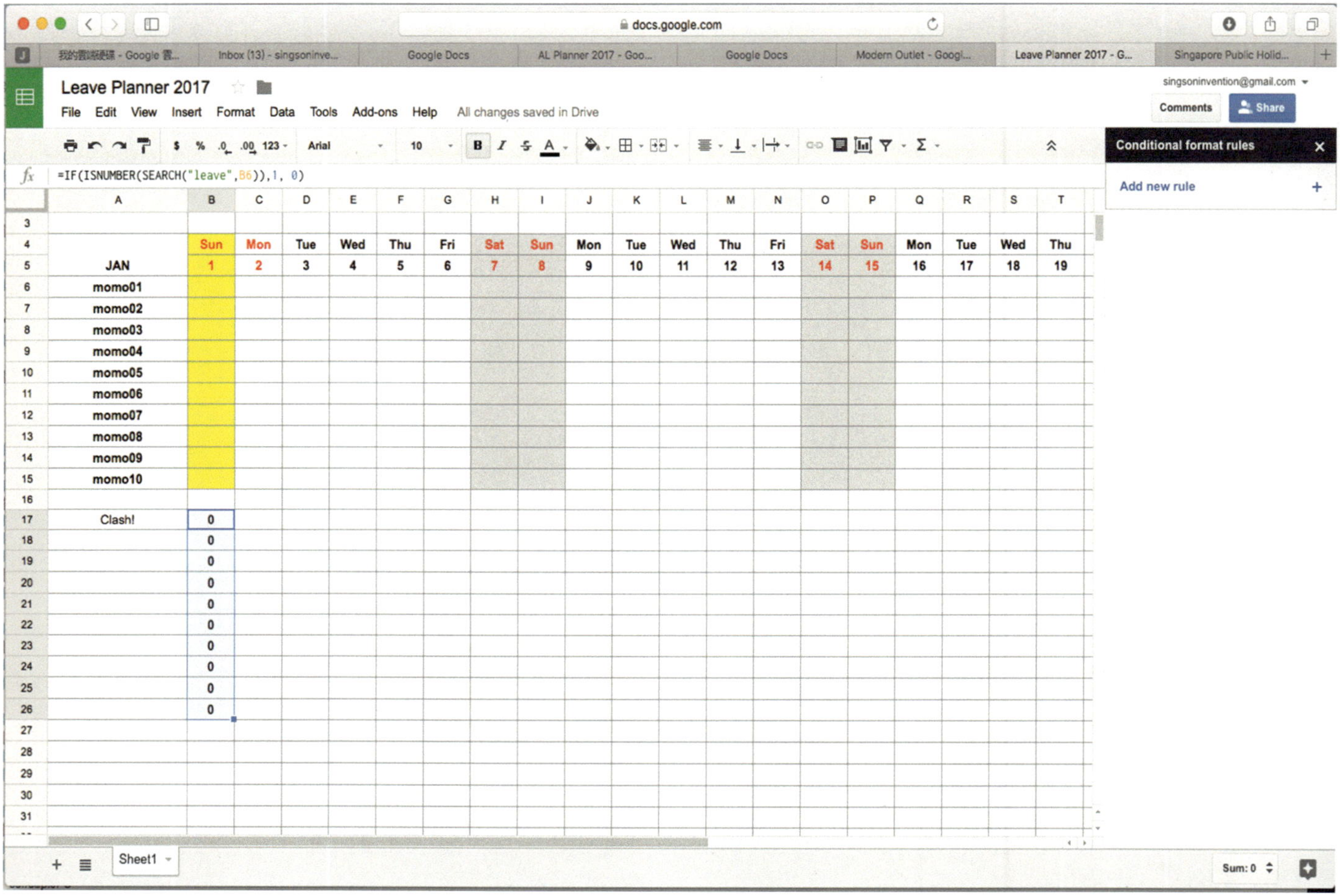

Set up auto-counting function of "leave" for all other staff on 01-Jan

1. Set up auto-count for "leave" for momo02 to momo10 for 01-Jan
2. Left click cell B17
3. Move mouse pointer to right lower corner of cell B17 until seeing "+"
4. Left click the "+" and hold and drag to B26, then release

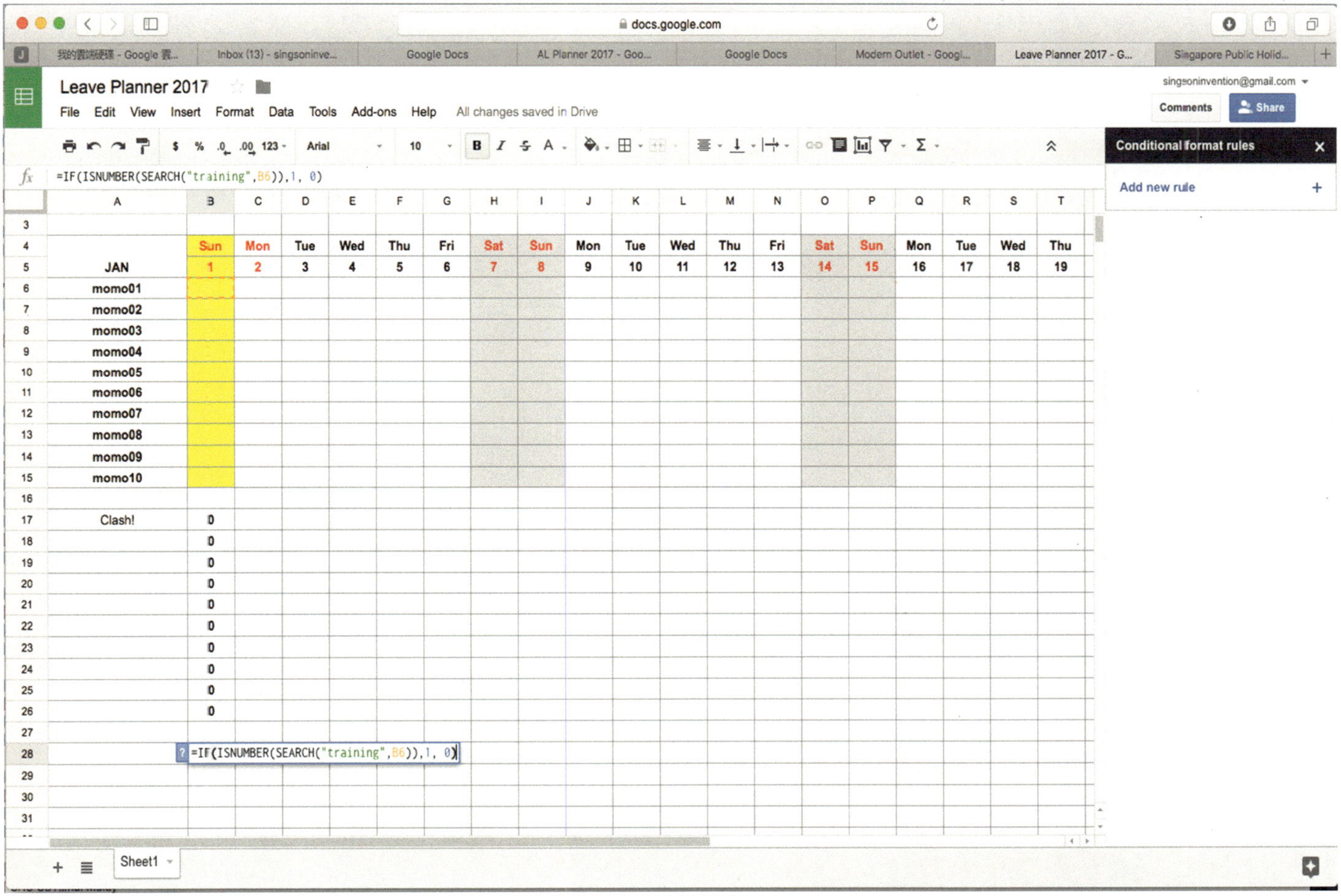

Set up auto-counting function of "training" for staff momo01 on 01-Jan

Set up auto-count for "training" for momo01 for 01-Jan → Left double click on cell B28 → Type in formula **=IF(ISNUMBER (SEARCH("training", B6)),1,0** → Press Enter upon completion

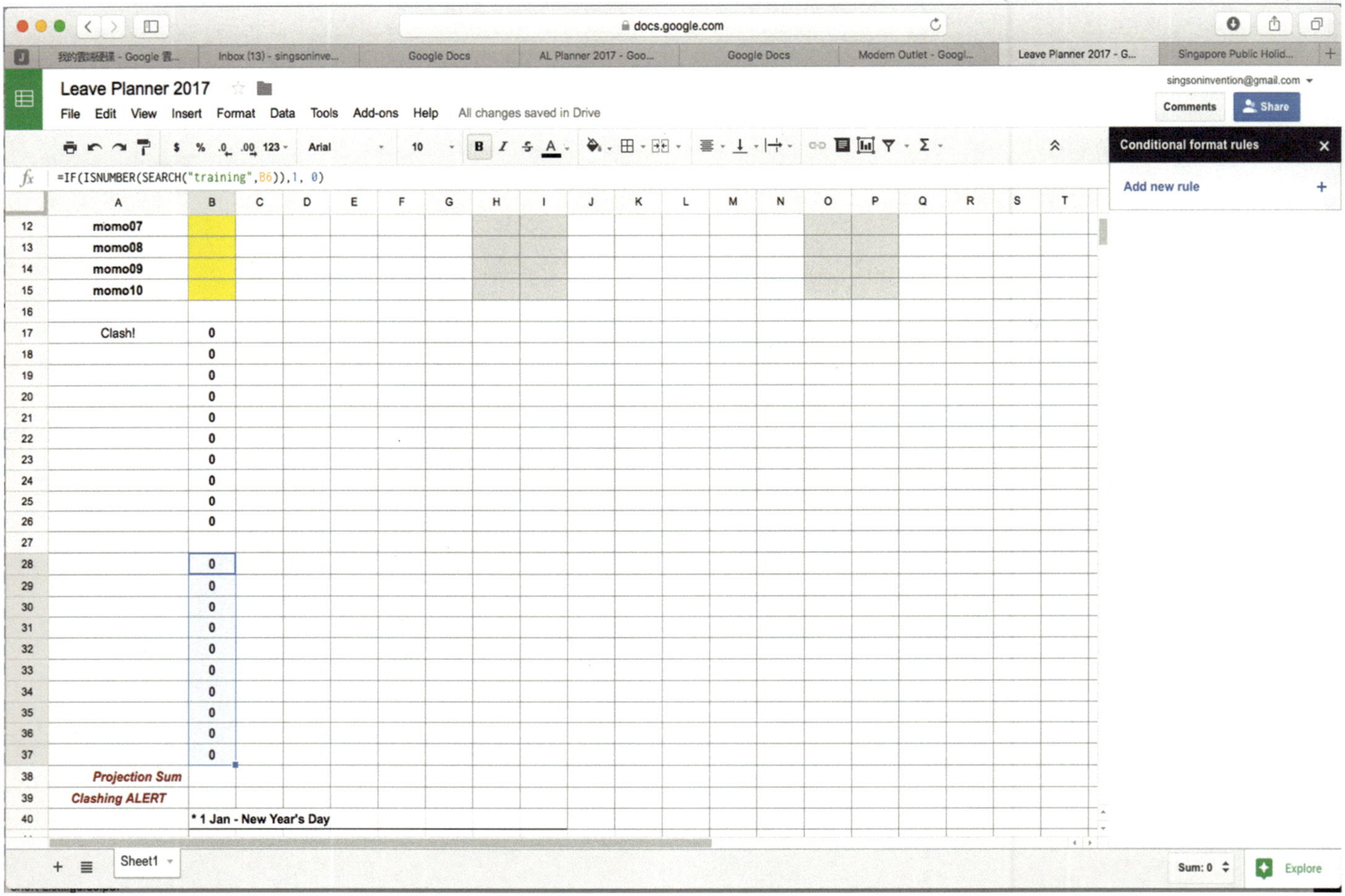

Set up auto-counting function of "training" for all other staff on 01-Jan

1. Set up auto-count for "training" for momo02 to momo10 for 01-Jan
2. Left click cell B28
3. Move mouse pointer to right lower corner of cell B28 until seeing "+"
4. Left click the "+" and hold and drag to B37, then release

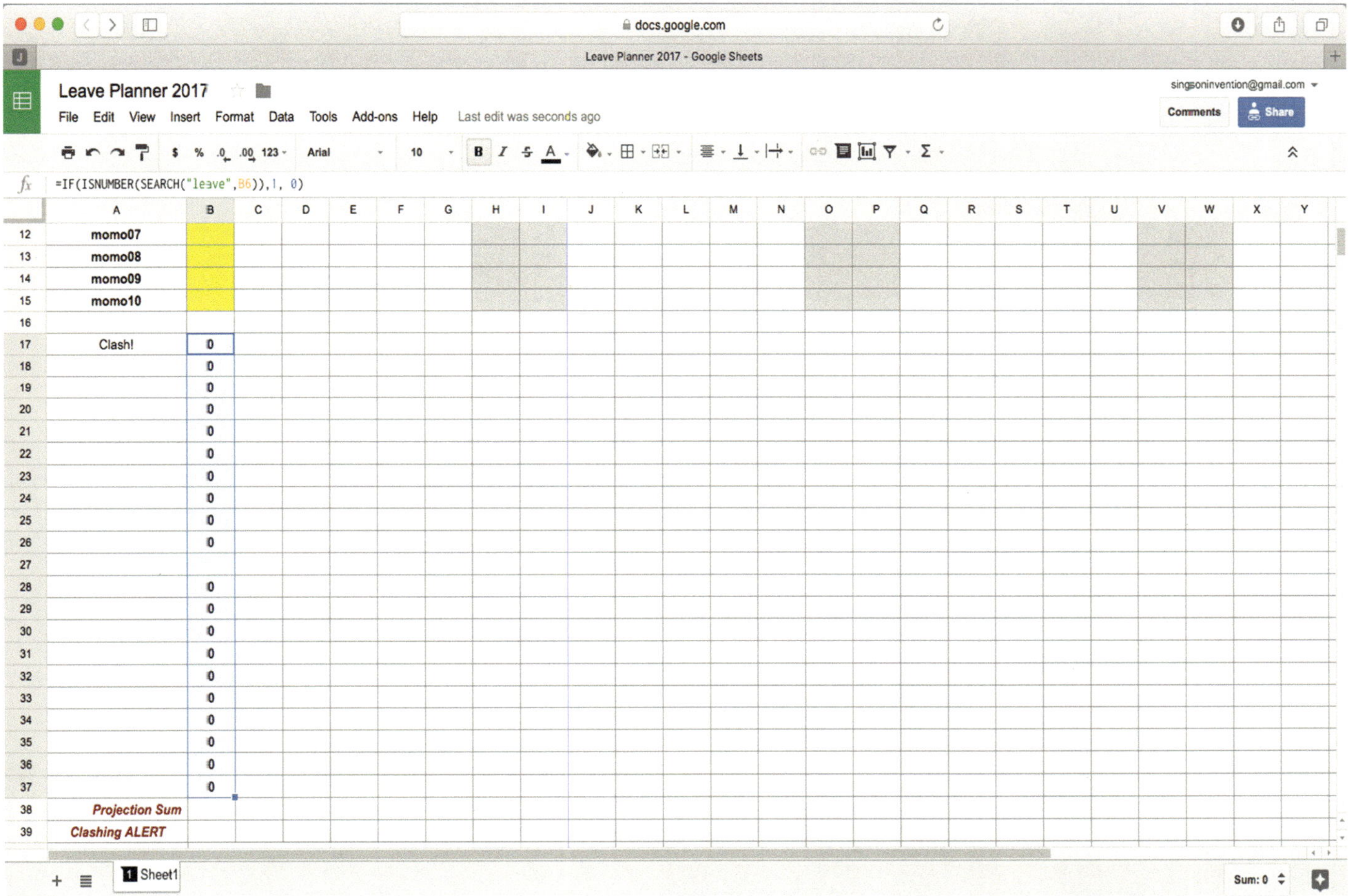

Extend auto-counting function of "leave" and "training" for all staff on all dates

Left click and hold to select cells B17 to B37

Move mouse pointer to right lower corner of cell B37 until seeing "+"

Left click the "+" and hold and drag to AF37 (i.e. 31-Jan), then release

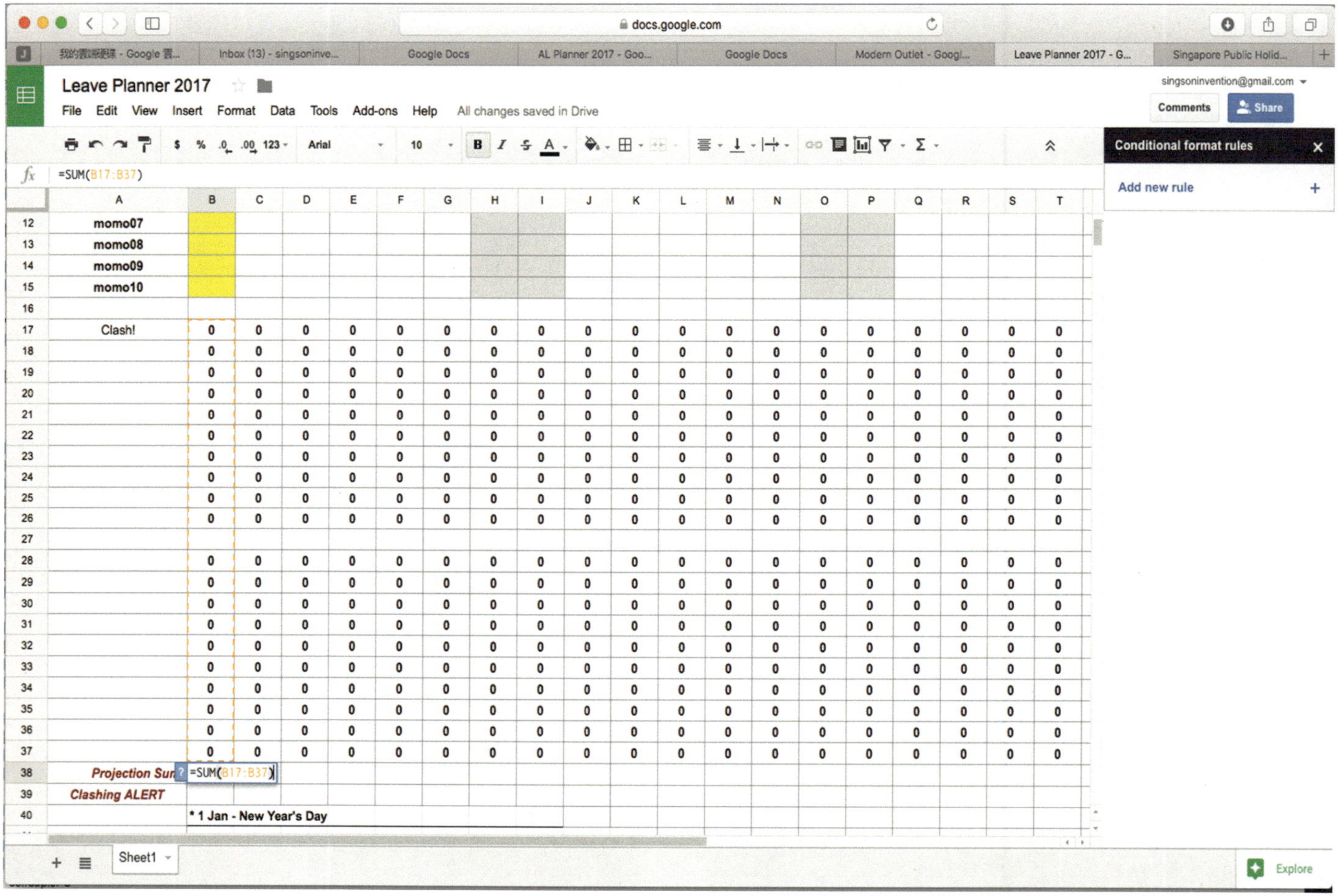

Set up sum function to add all "training" and "leave" projection for all staff on all dates

1. Left double click cell B38
2. Type in formula =SUM(B17:B37)
3. Press Enter upon completion

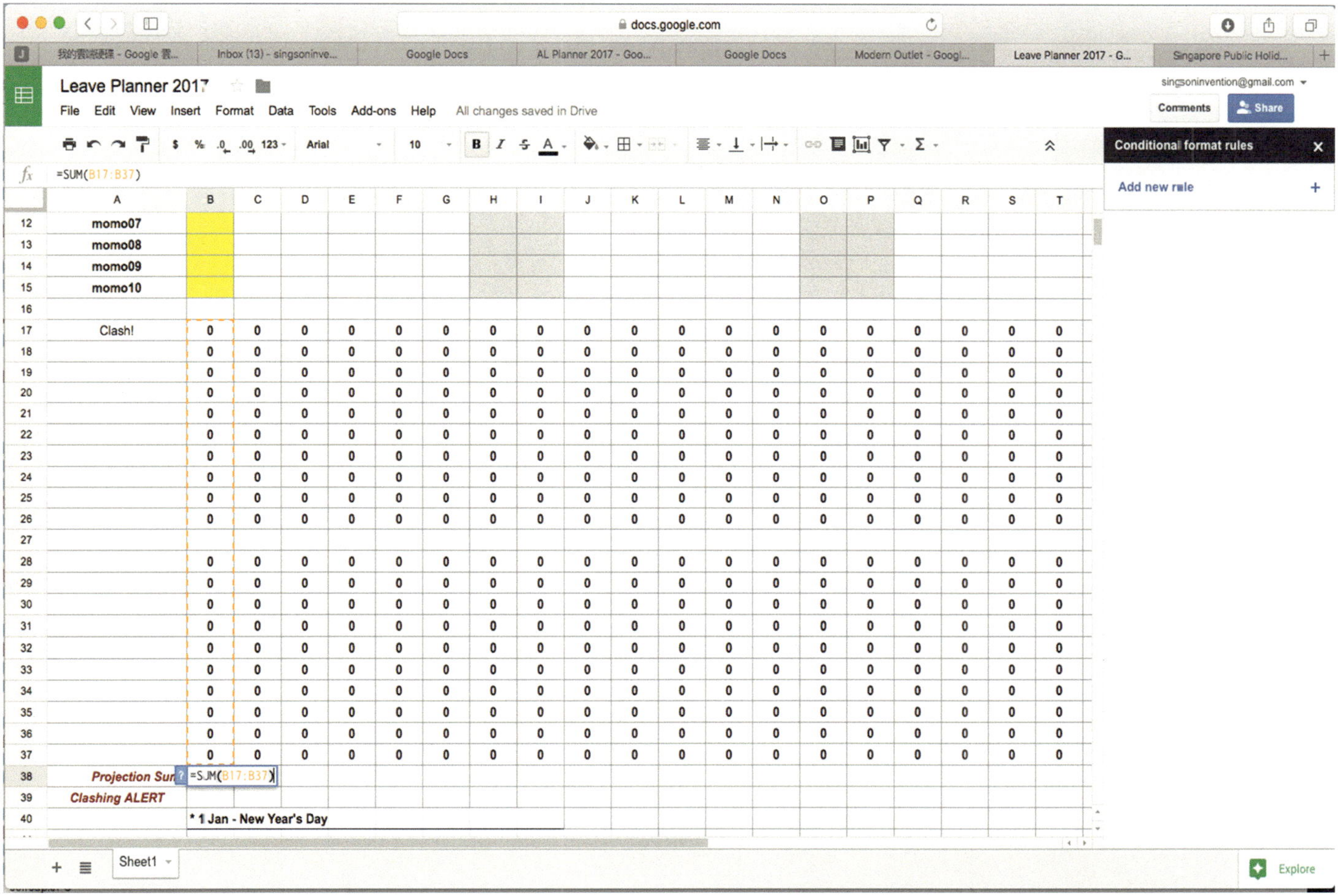

Set up sum function to add all "training" and "leave" projection for all staff on all dates

Left click cell B38, click the "+" and hold and drag to AF38

Left double click cell A38 and type "Projection sum"

Left double click cell A17 and type "Clash!"

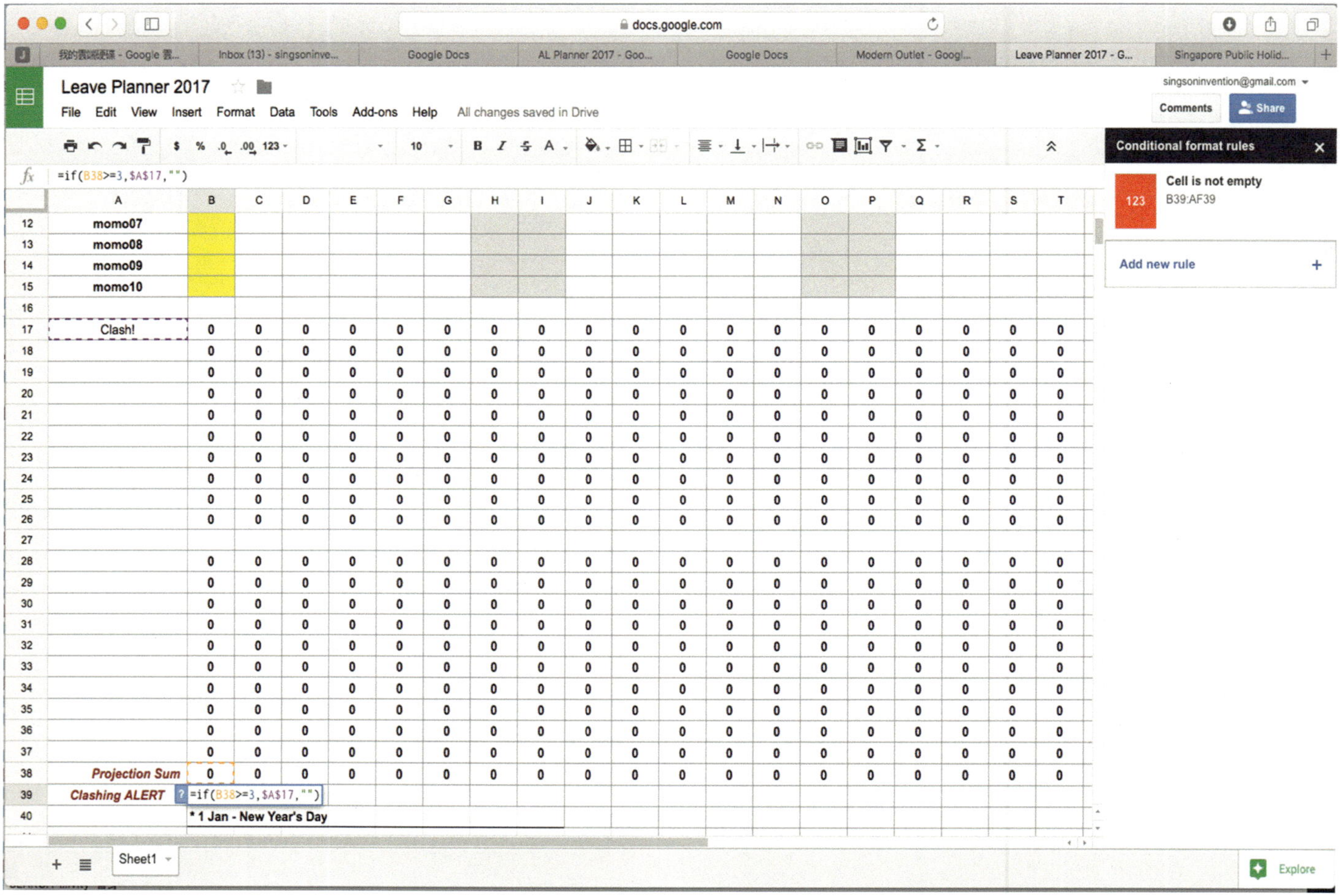

Set up Clash alert function to monitor clashes i.e. more than 2 staff going on leave or training on the same day in our setting

1. Left double click cell B39
2. Type in formula =IF(B38=>3, A17,"")
3. Press Enter upon completion
4. Left click cell B39, click the "+" and hold and drag to AF39

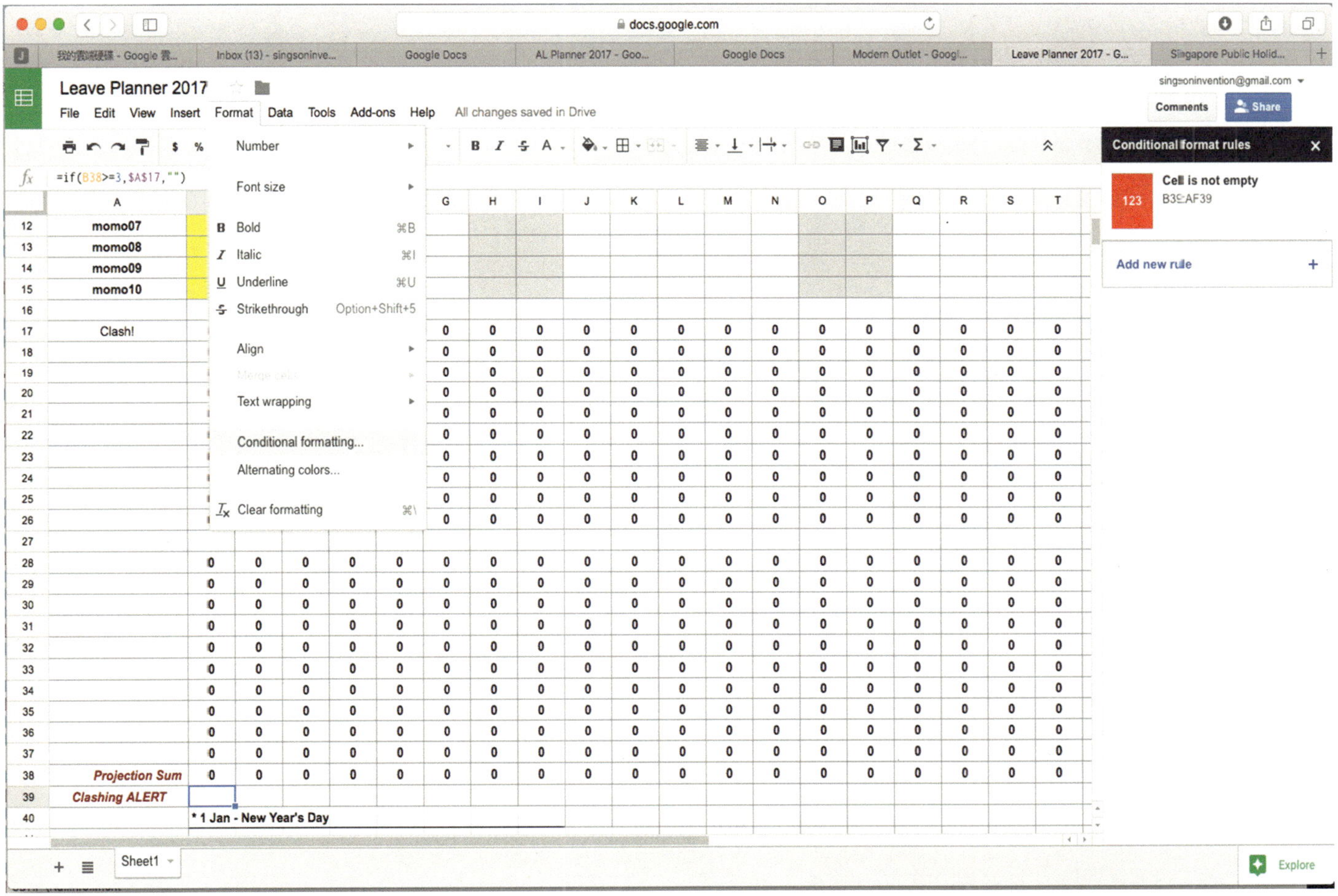

Set up Conditional formatting to highlight the Clash alert in the event it happens

Left click and hold to select cells B39 to AF39 → Go to toolbar → Left click "Format" → Left click "Conditional formatting"

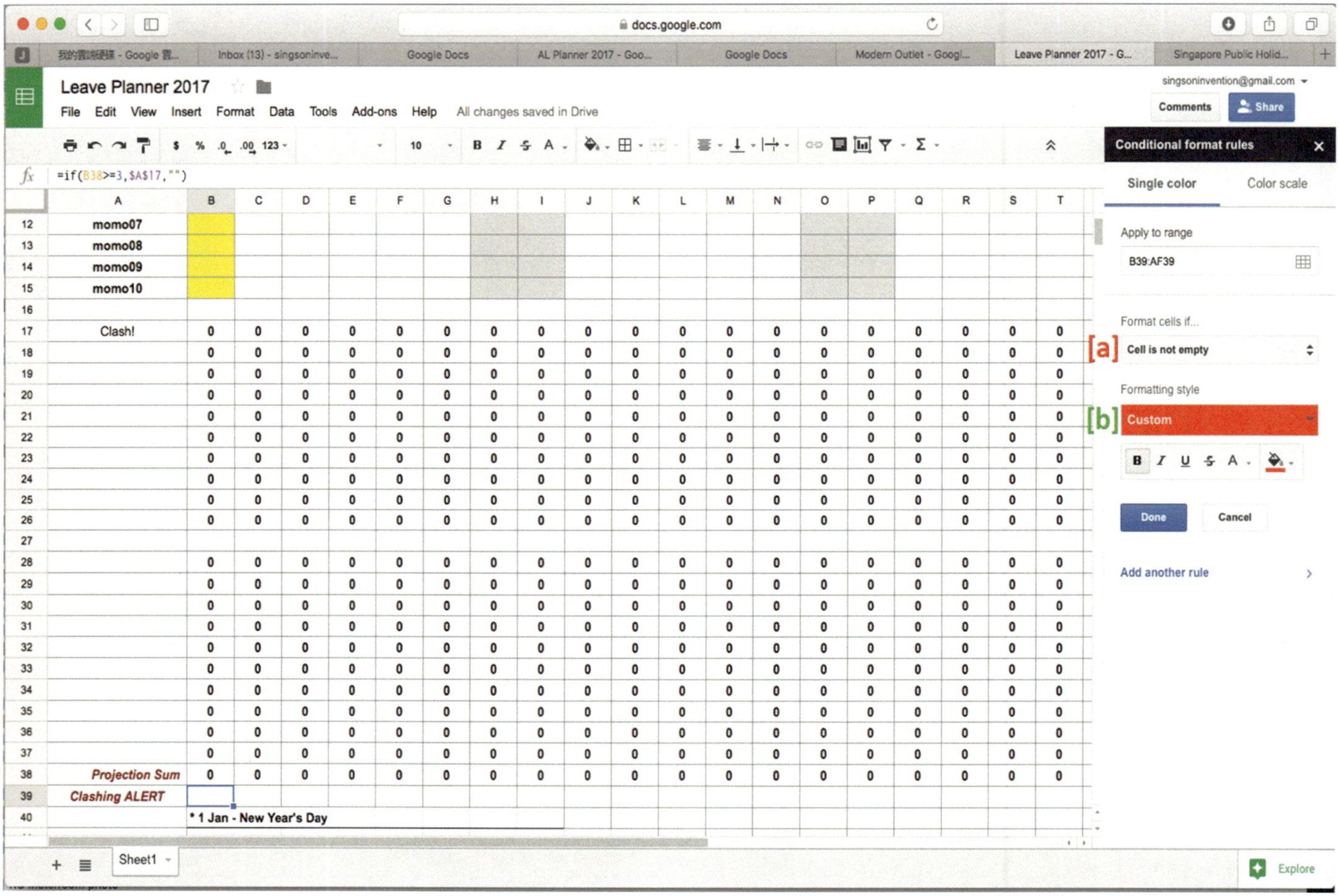

Configure Conditional formatting rules

1. Left click **[a]** to choose the condition (e.g. Cell is not empty)
2. Choose the Formatting style in **[b]** (e.g. words in white, bond, and background in red)
3. Press "Done" upon completion

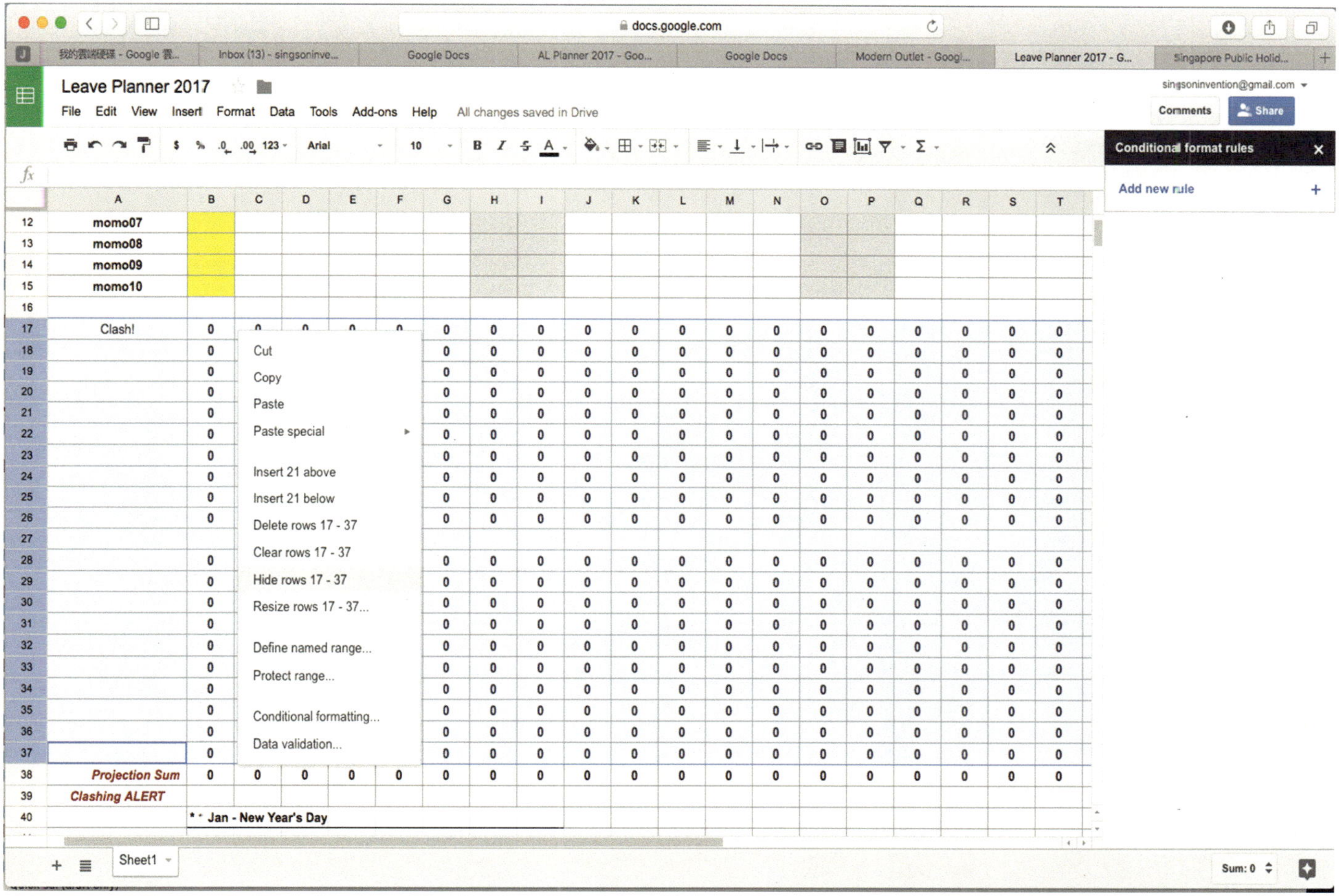

Hide the auto-counting rows to make them invisible

Left click row 17 to 37 and hold to select them → Right click to show the menu → Left click "Hide rows 17-37

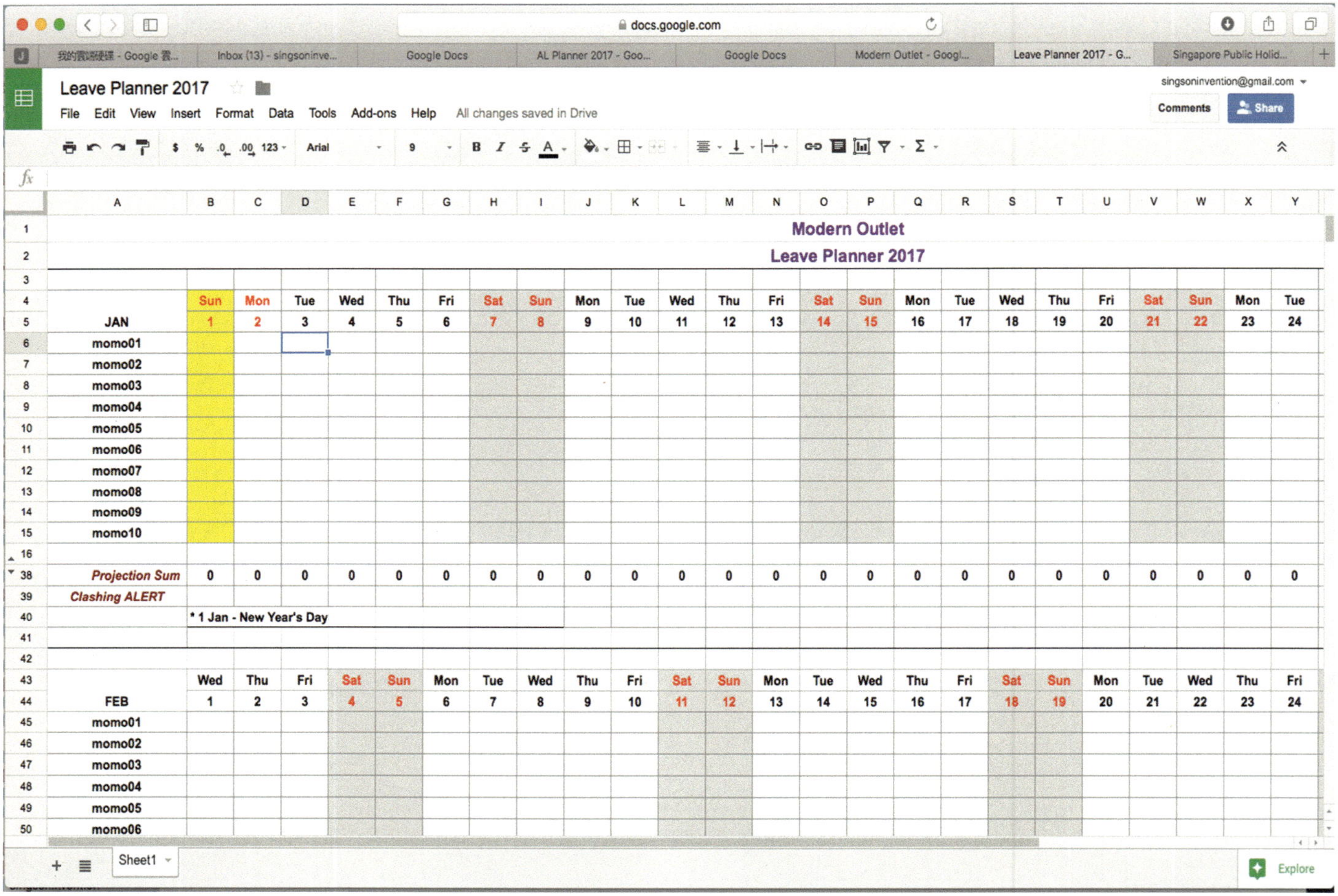

Repeat the previous steps described in P.8-25 for the months of Feb to Dec to complete the whole calendar

Go to P.8 of this guide to create the calendar of Feb, including dates and staff

Refer to P.9-13 to set up conditional formatting rules; require to change the relative cells position accordingly

Refer to P.14-25 to set of clash alert; require to change the relative cells position accordingly

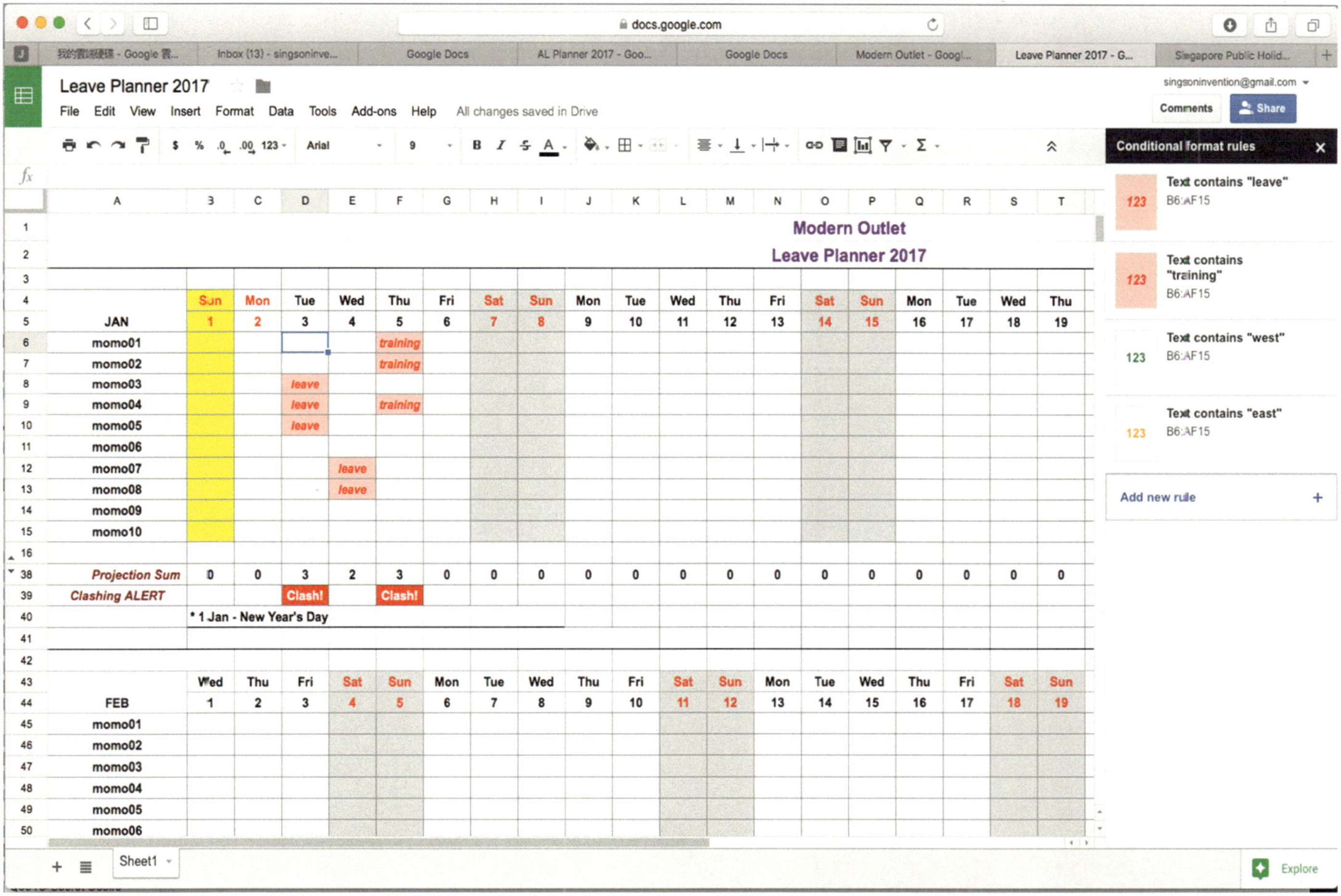

Test the Conditional formatting and Clash alert functions

Type "leave" and "training" to the cells as displayed above

"leave" and "training" will be highlighted in red, bond and italic

Projection sum on 3-Jan, 4-Jan and 5-Jan will be shown as 3, 2, 3

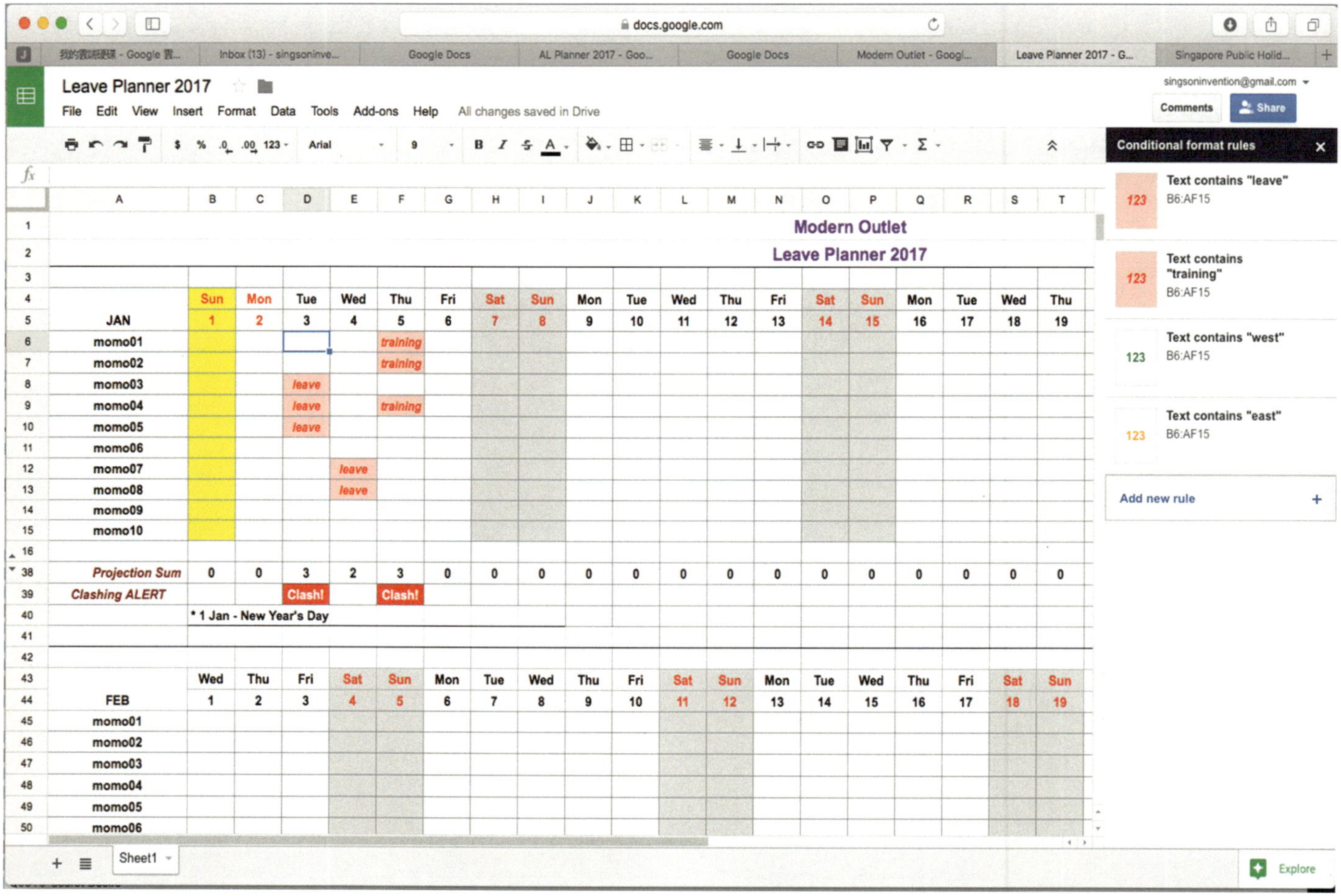

Test the Conditional formatting and Clash alert functions

When projection is more than 2, Clash alert will be activated

"Clash!" are shown for 3-Jan and 5-Jan due to clashing

"Clash!" is in white, bond with red in background

Chapter 4)

Change sharing setting to allow staff for editing

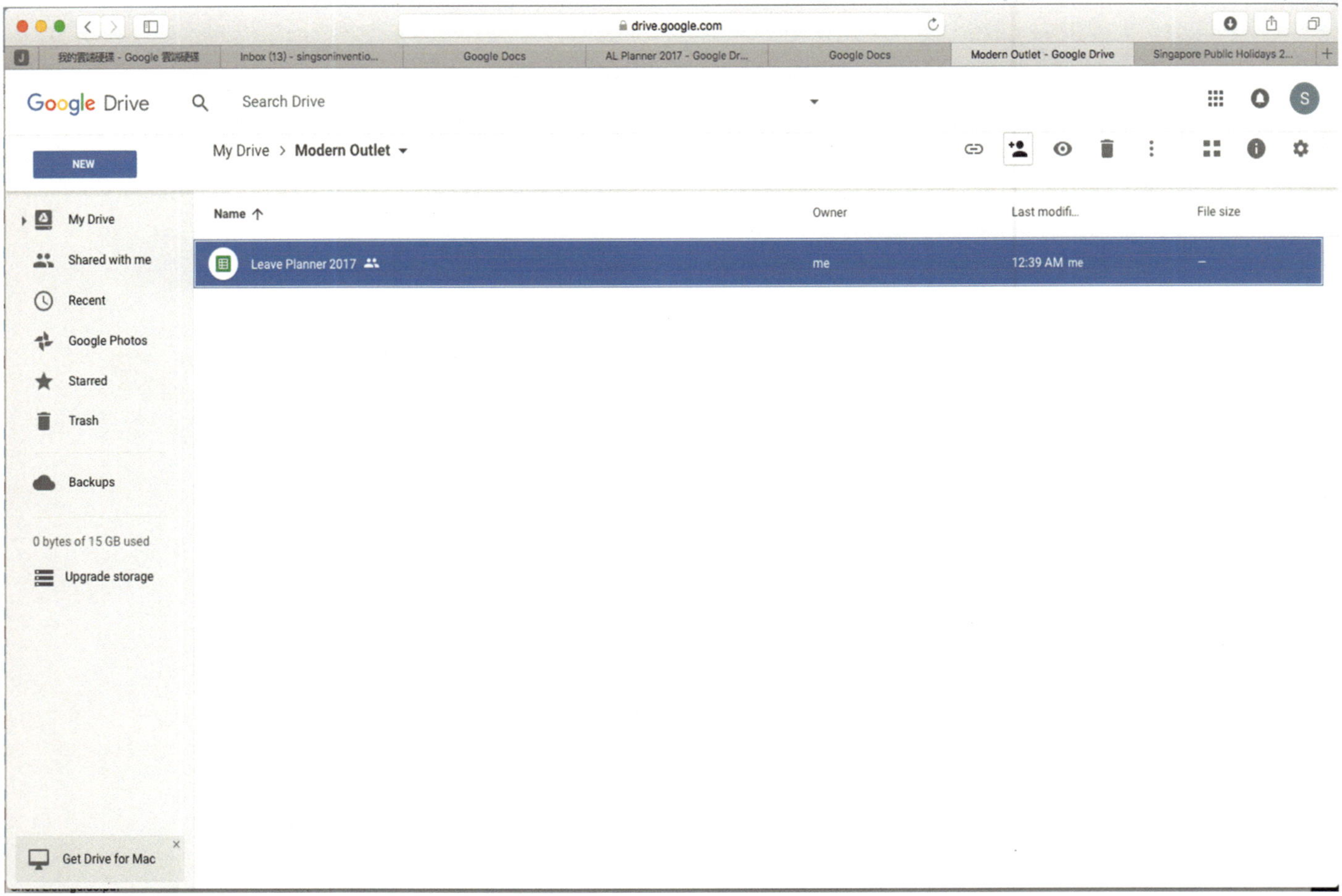

 # Once the set up of the whole calendar is completed, you can change the setting to assign editing right to you staff

Change of sharing setting so that staff can log in and edit

Right click the Sheets file – Leave Planner 2017 → Left click "Share"

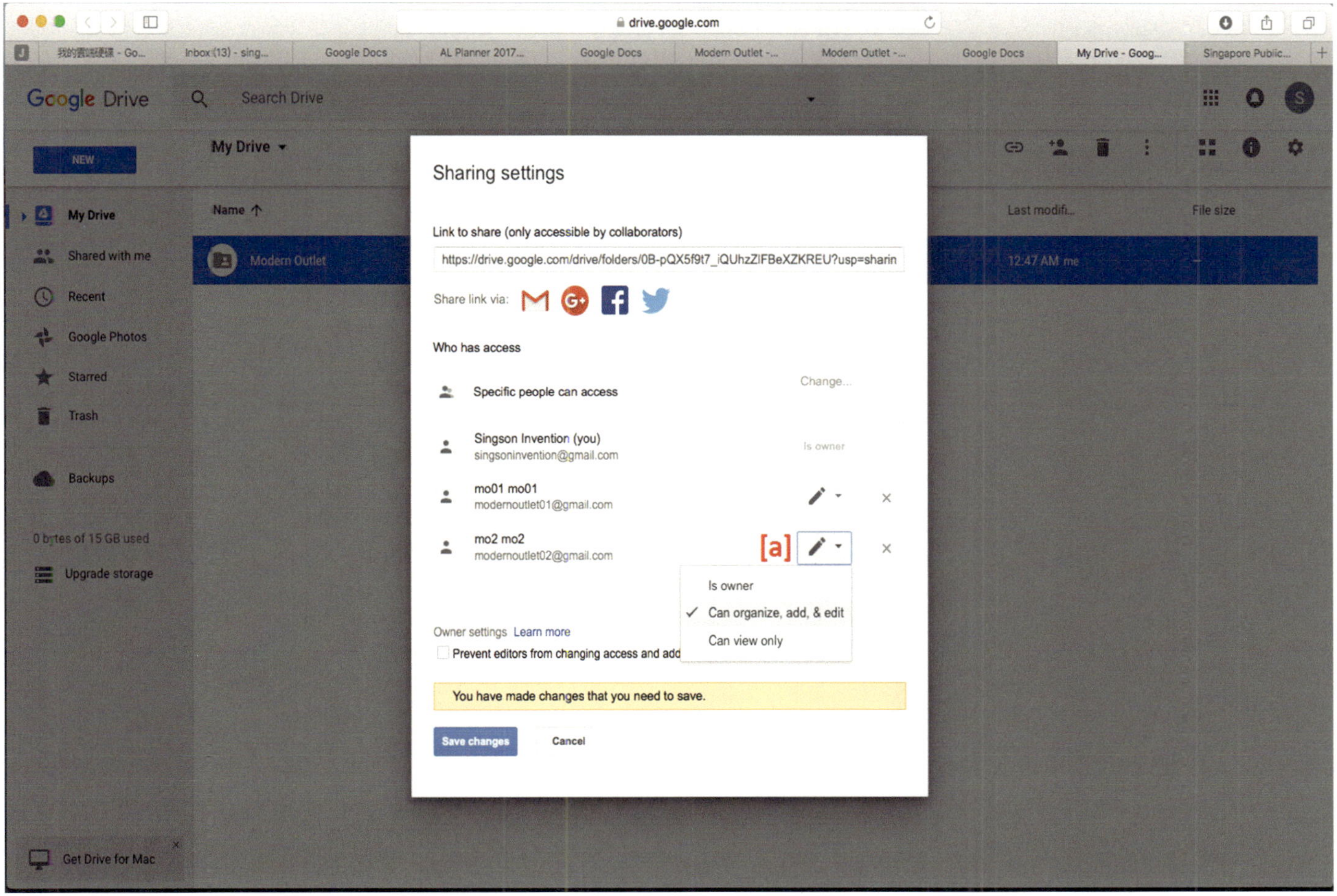

Change of sharing setting so that staff can log in and edit

1. Left click **[a]** to choose "Can organise, add & edit"
2. Repeat for all staff to allow editing access
3. Press "Save changes" upon completion

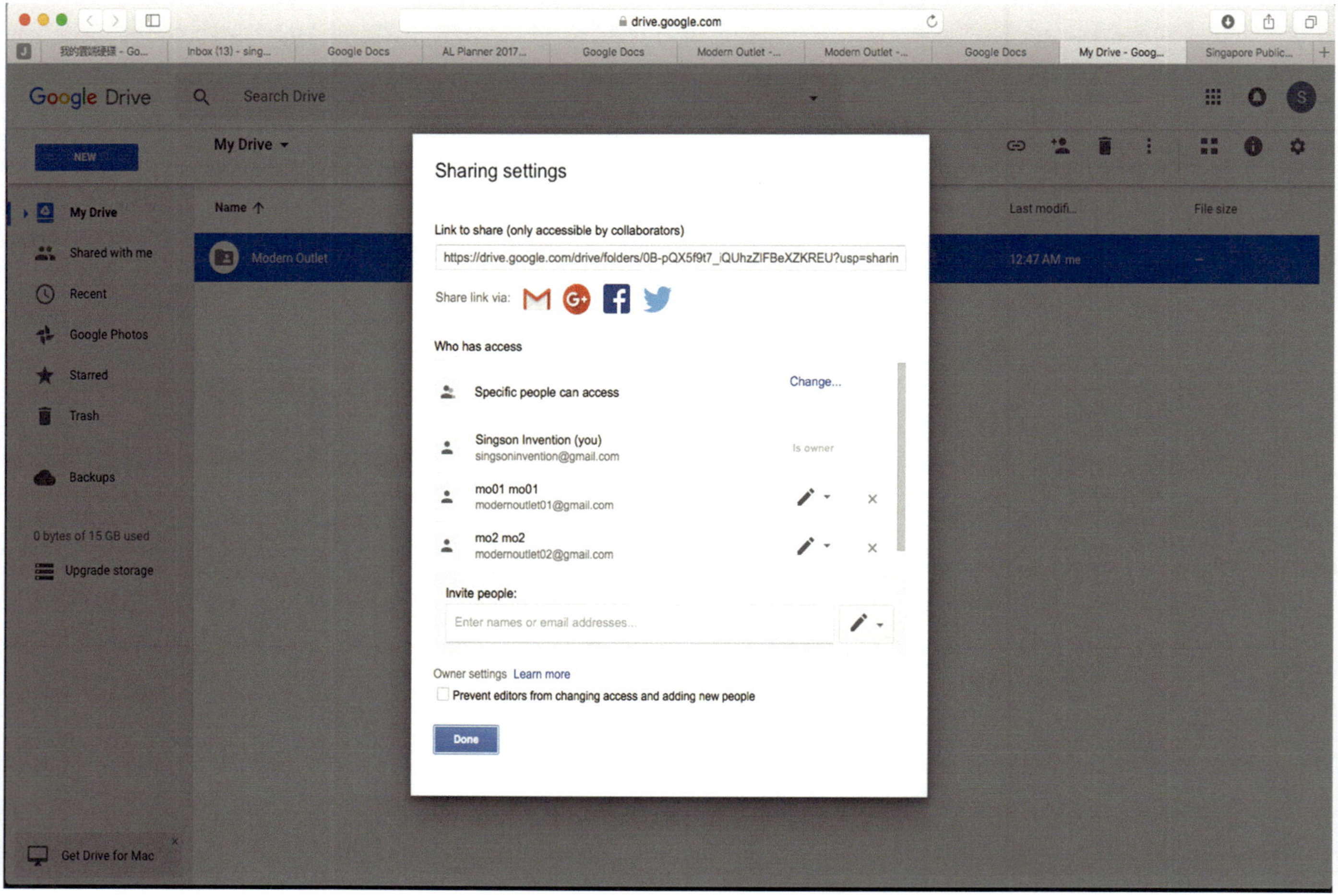

Change of sharing setting so that staff can log in and edit

Ensure all staff are given edit access (Pencil symbol)

Press "Done" upon completion

Chapter 5)

Set up staff-specific editing permissions for cells and rows

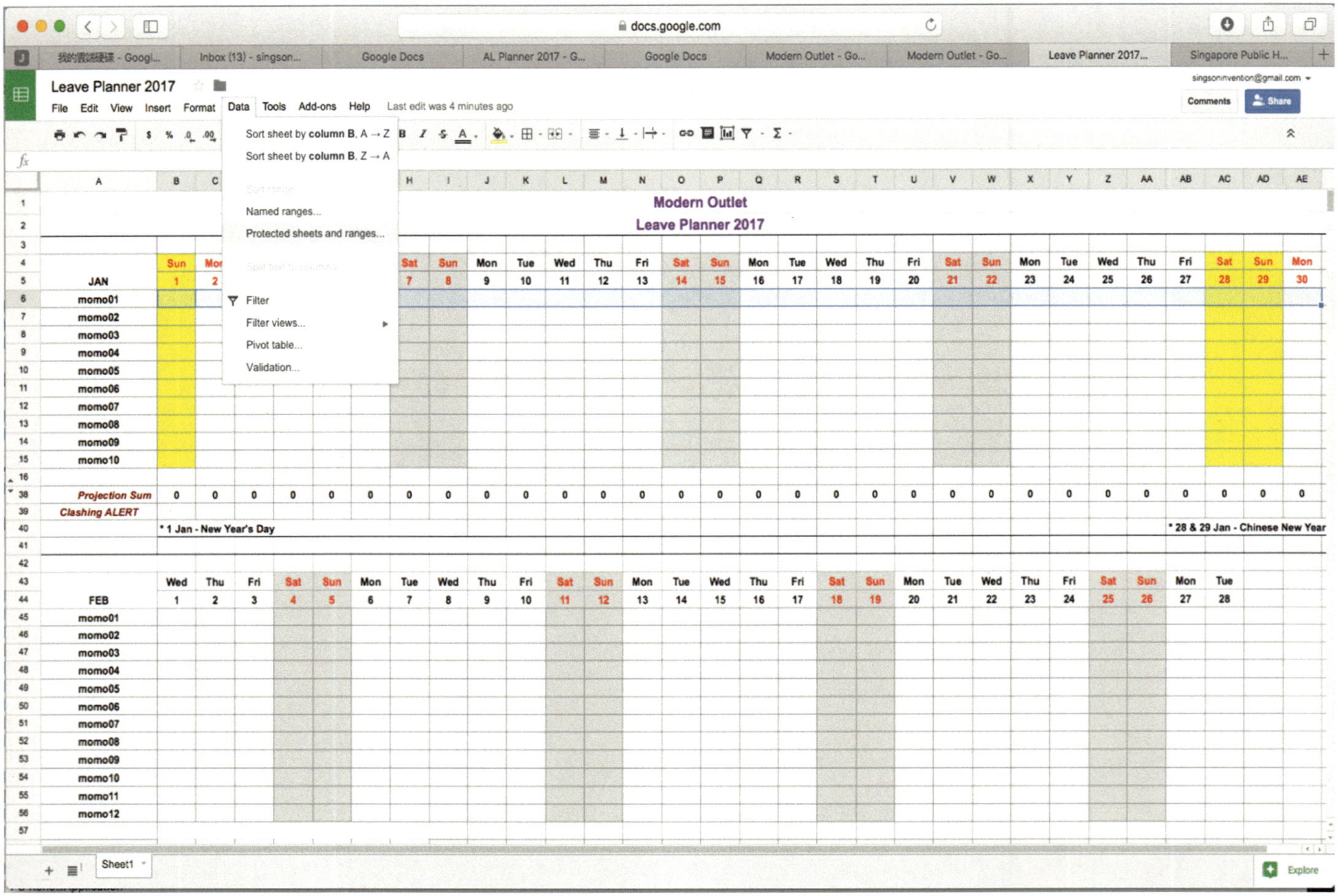

 # After giving access and edit right of the Sheets file to staff, the next step is to configure the edit permissions of different cells and rows

Set up staff-specific editing permissions for certain cells and rows

Left click and hold to select cell B6 to AF6 → Go to toolbar → Left click "Protected sheets and ranges"

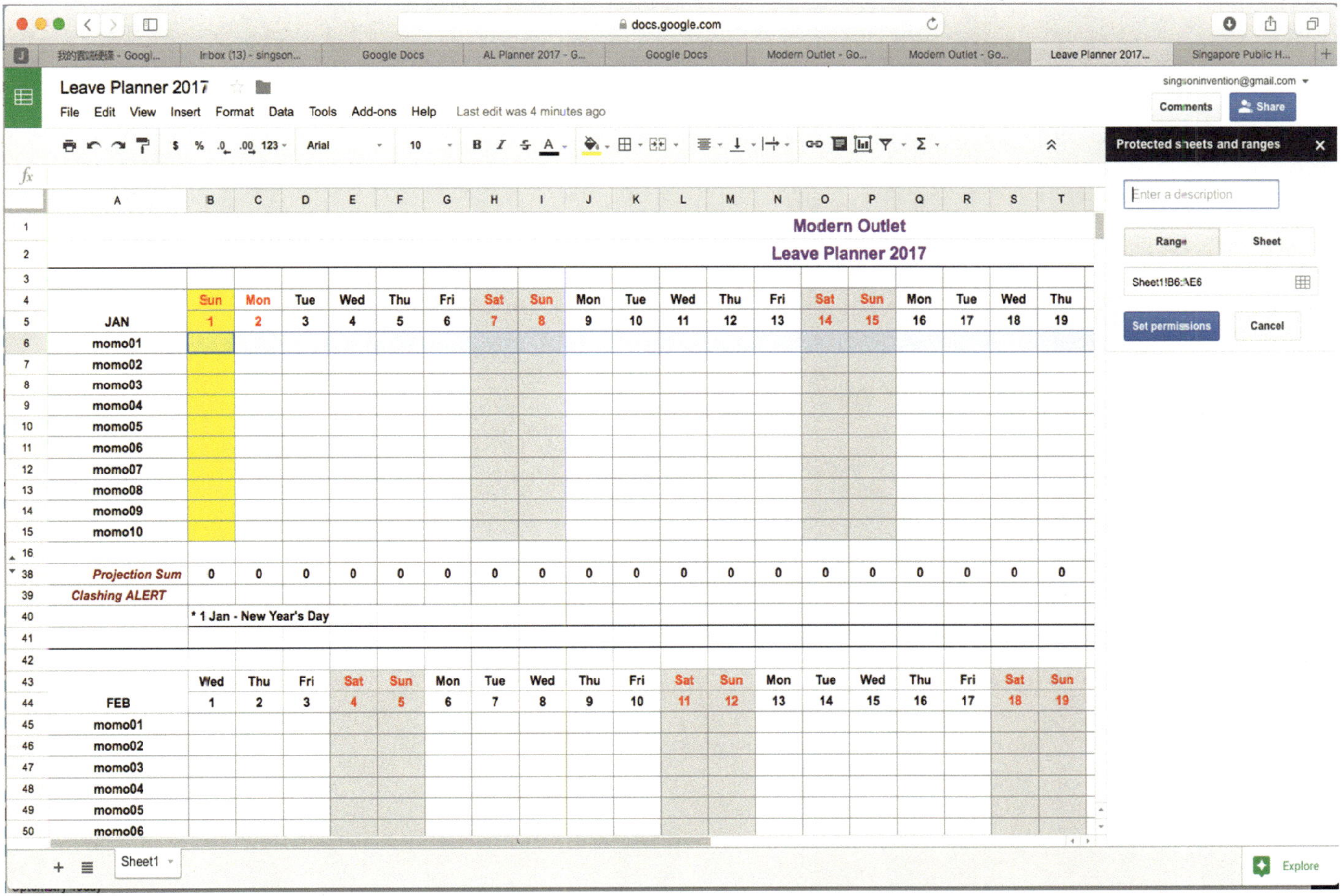

Set permissions for staff momo01

Go to the right menu → Press "Set permissions"

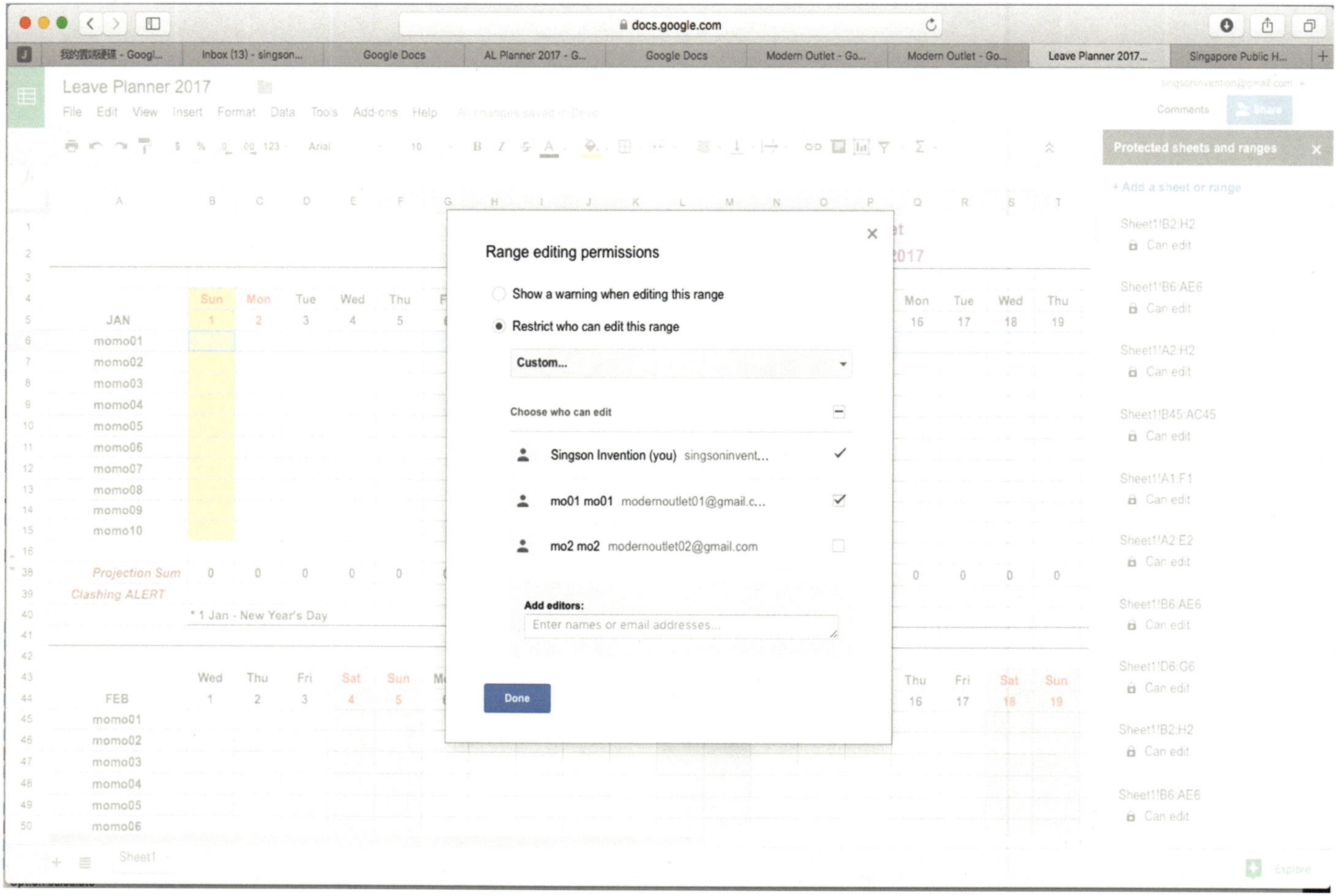

Set permissions for staff momo01

1. Leave the checked box for staff momo01 remains "tick"
2. Left click to "untick" the checked boxes for other staff
3. Press "Done" upon completion

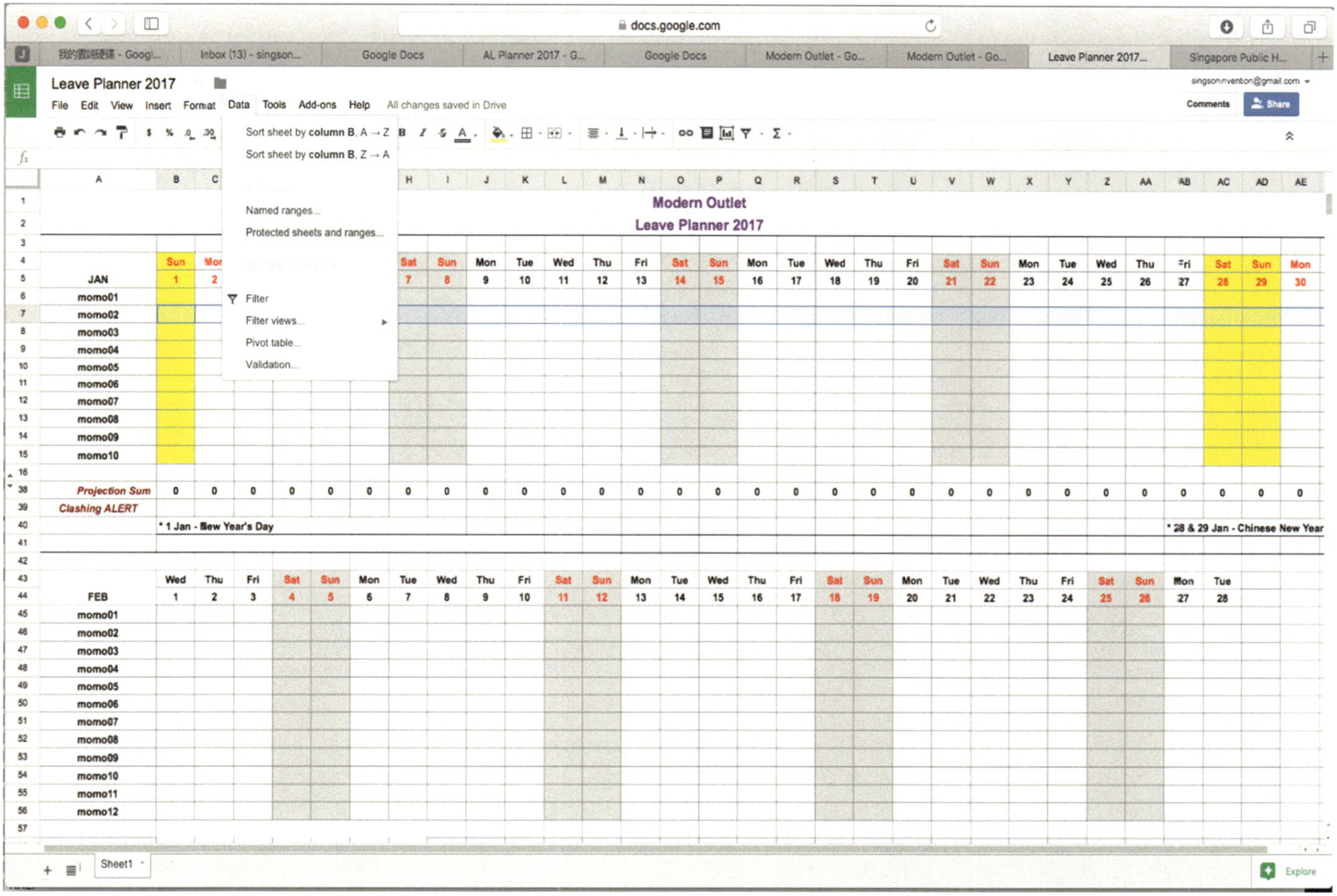

Set permissions for staff momo02 and other staff

1. Left click and hold to select cell C7 to AF7
2. Go to toolbar
3. Left click "Protected sheets and ranges
4. Press "Set permissions"

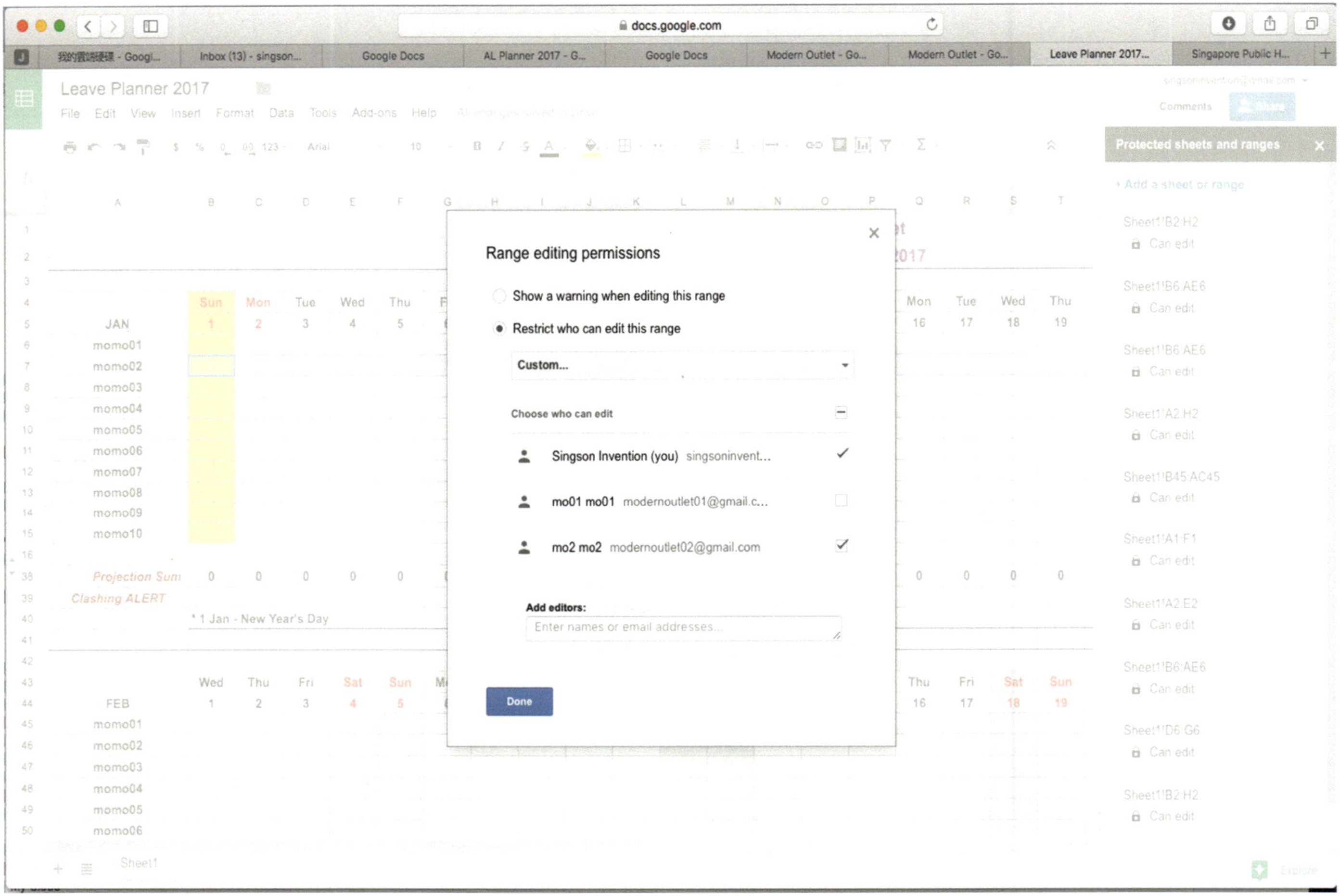

Set permissions for staff momo02 and other staff

1. Let the checked box for staff momo02 remains "tick"
2. Left click to "untick" the checked boxes for other staff
3. Press "Done" upon completion
4. Repeat the above for all staff in Jan and do the same for all months

Chapter 6)

Staff Log in for editing
(Staff to indicate their leave request)

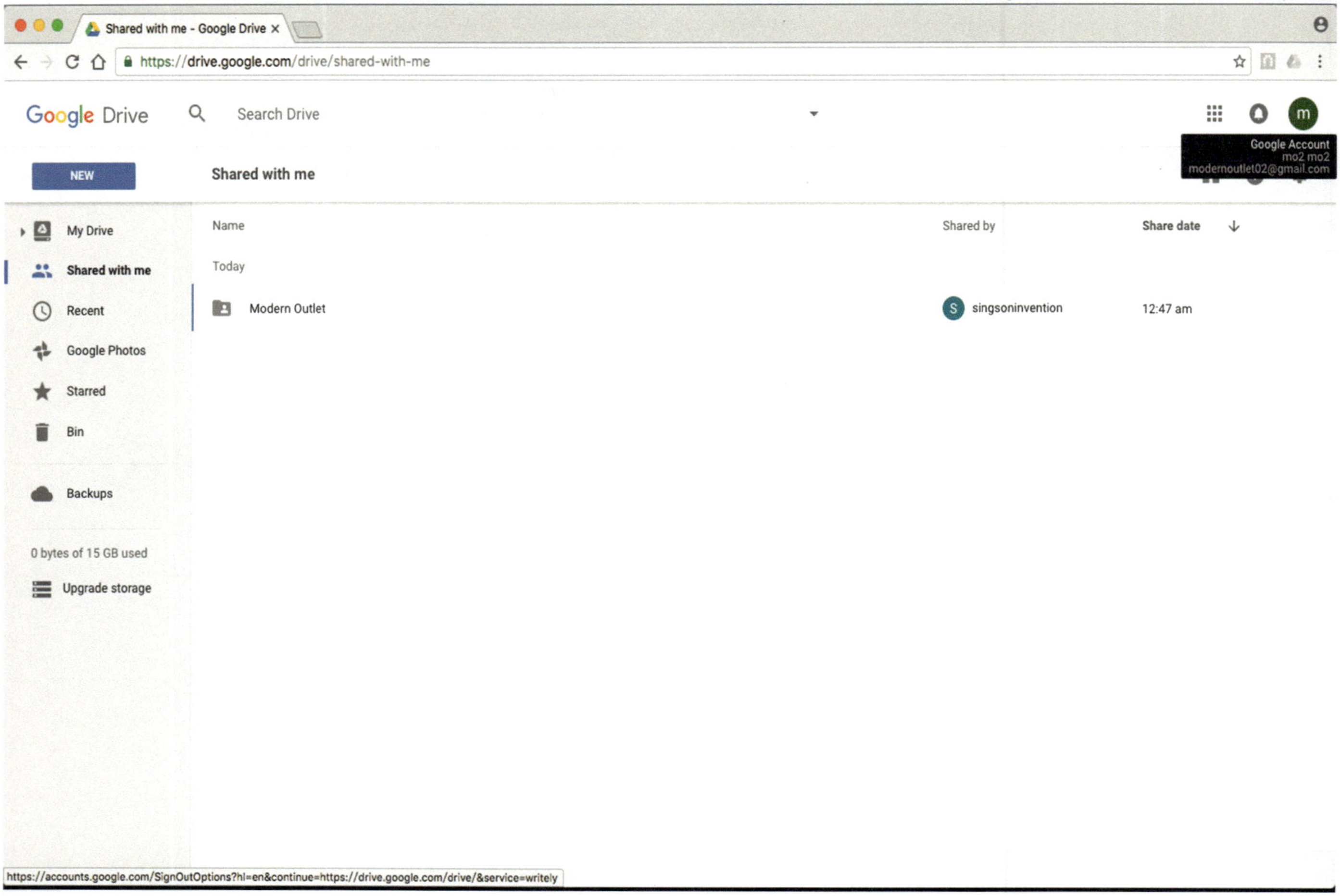

 # The set up of the whole calendar is completed after Chapter 5. Now the planner is ready for staff to use

Staff momo02 log in to his Google Drive to edit the Leave Planner

Left click "Shared with me"

Left double click the folder "Modern Outlet"

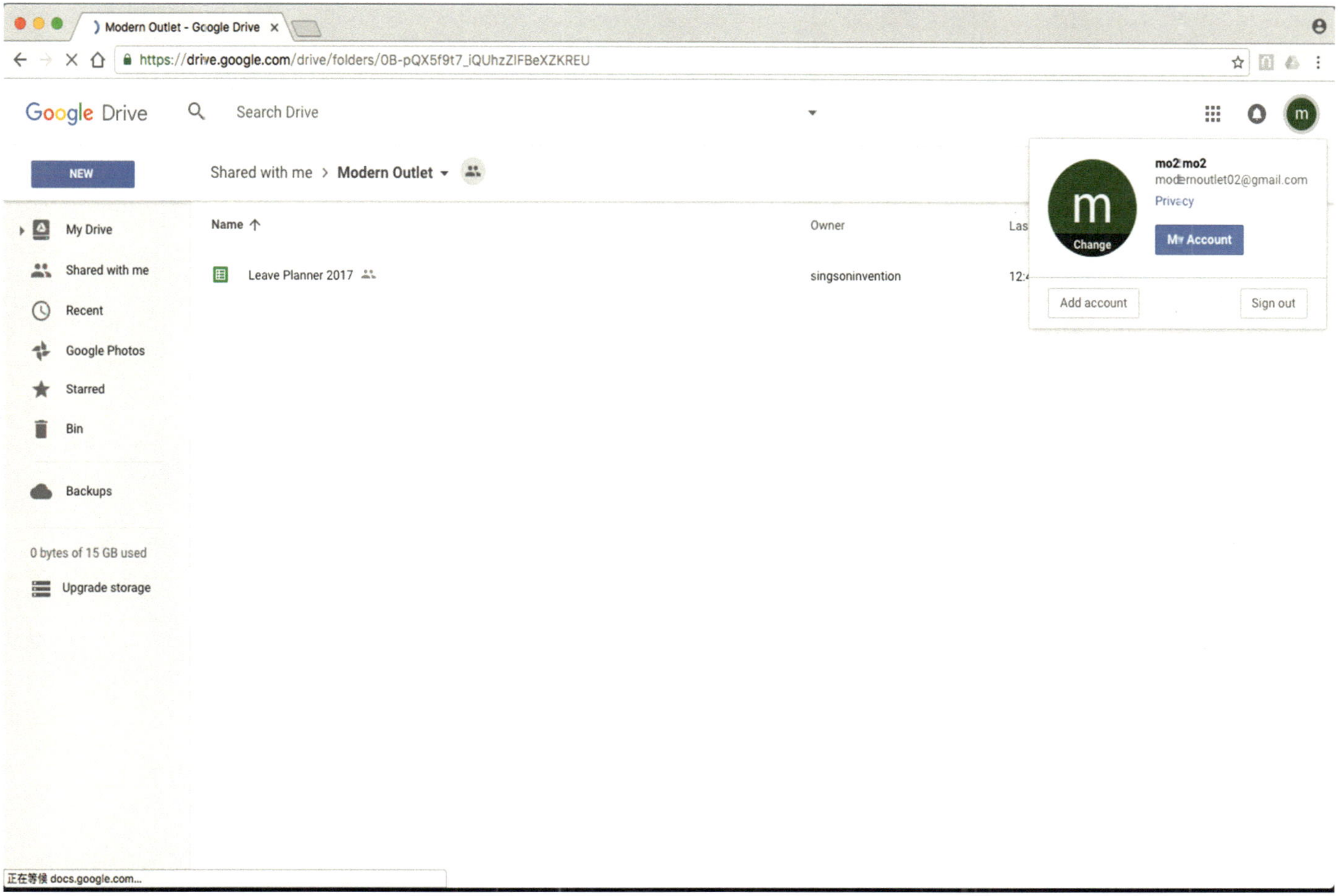

Staff momo02 log in to his Google Drive to edit the Leave Planner

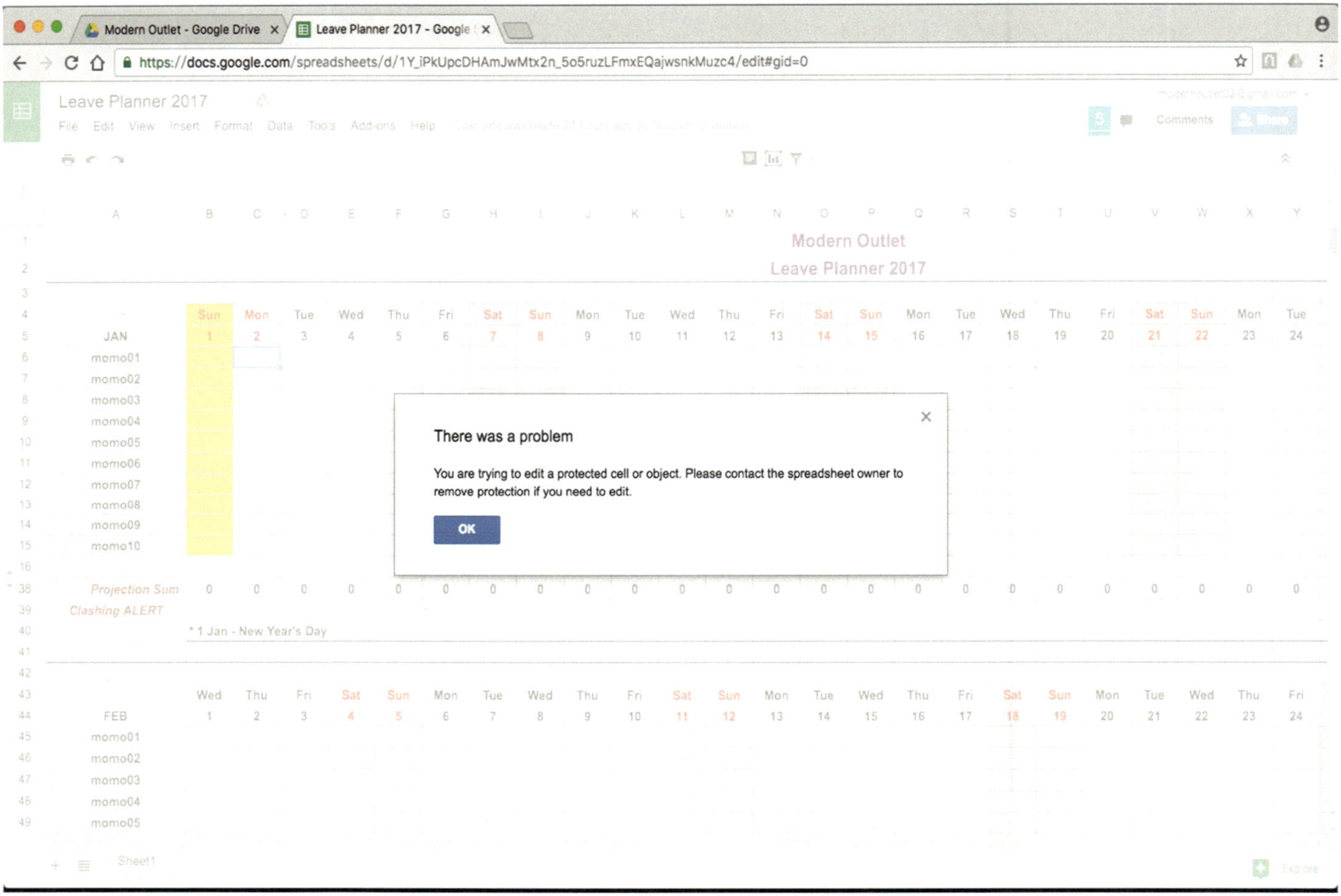

Staff can only edit the cells that he has been given permissions

When staff momo02 clicks on the cell C6 that belongs to momo01

An error message will be popped up

Staff momo02 cannot edit on cells that belong to other staff

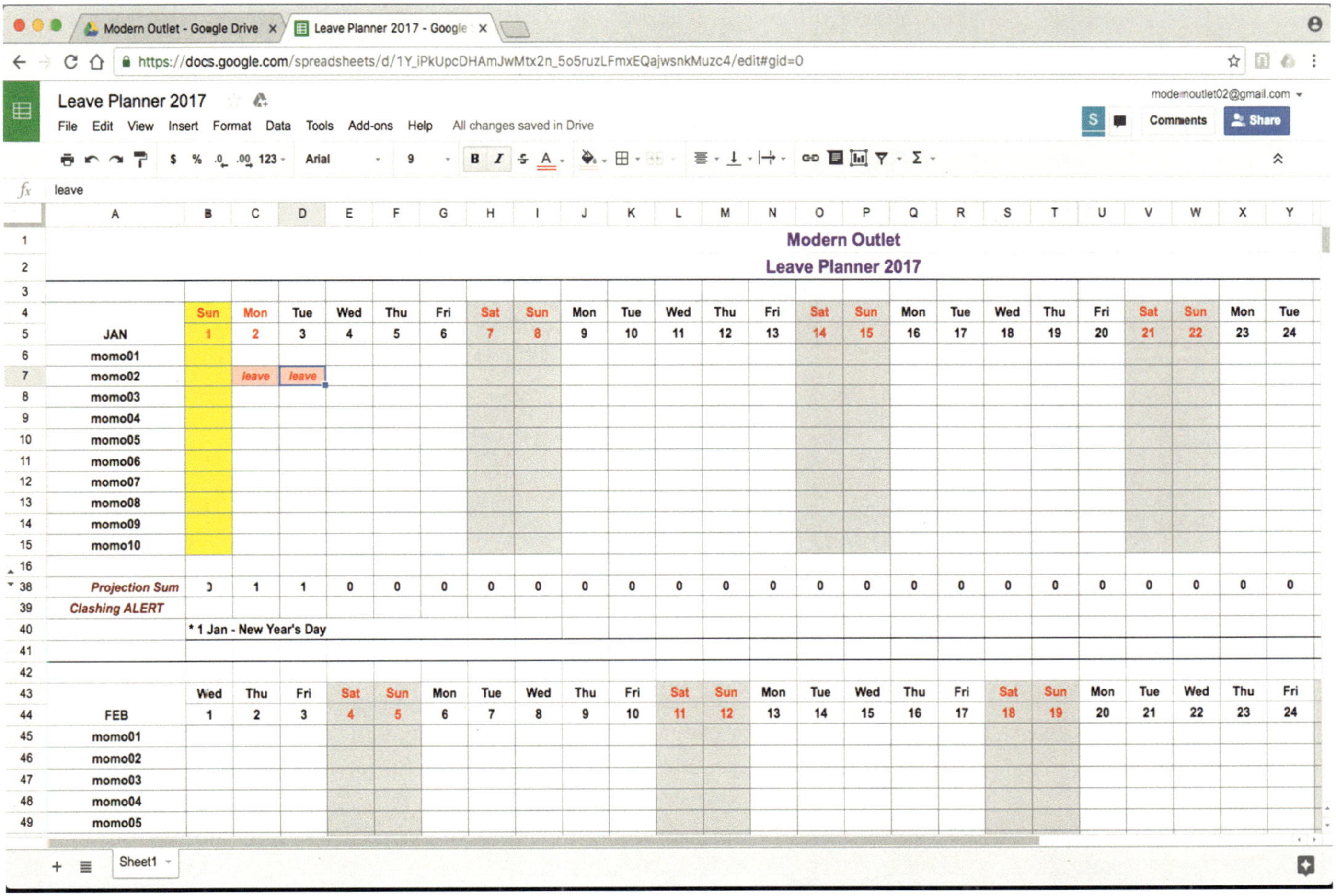

Staff can only edit the cells that he has been given permissions

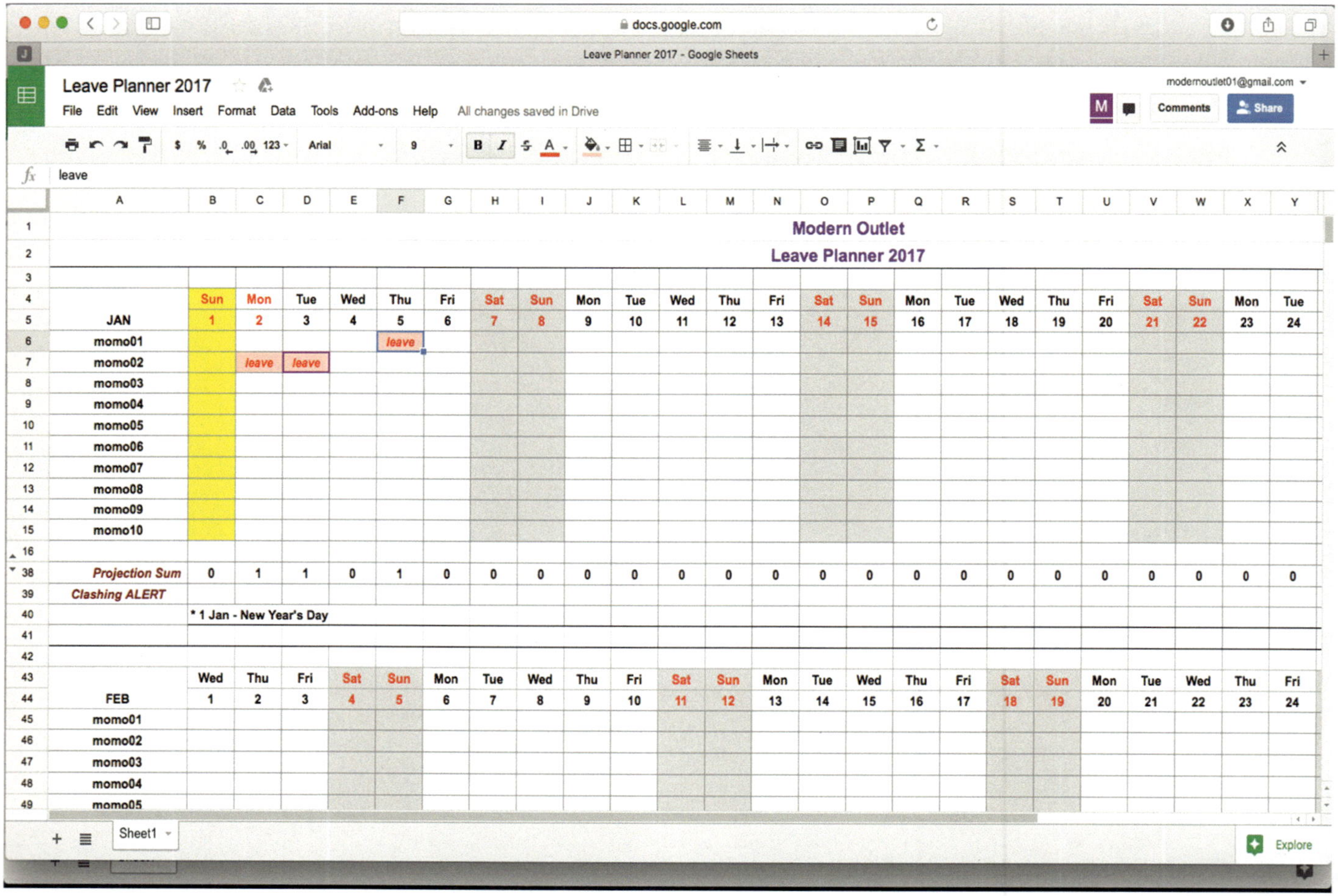

Modern Outlet

Leave Planner 2017

	A	B	C	D	E	F	G	H	I	J	K	L	M	N	O	P	Q	R	S	T	U	V	W	X	Y
4		Sun	Mon	Tue	Wed	Thu	Fri	Sat	Sun	Mon	Tue	Wed	Thu	Fri	Sat	Sun	Mon	Tue	Wed	Thu	Fri	Sat	Sun	Mon	Tue
5	JAN	1	2	3	4	5	6	7	8	9	10	11	12	13	14	15	16	17	18	19	20	21	22	23	24
6	momo01					leave																			
7	momo02		leave	leave																					
8	momo03																								
9	momo04																								
10	momo05																								
11	momo06																								
12	momo07																								
13	momo08																								
14	momo09																								
15	momo10																								
16																									
38	Projection Sum	0	1	1	0	1	0	0	0	0	0	0	0	0	0	0	0	0	0	0	0	0	0	0	0
39	Clashing ALERT																								
40		* 1 Jan - New Year's Day																							
43		Wed	Thu	Fri	Sat	Sun	Mon	Tue	Wed	Thu	Fri	Sat	Sun	Mon	Tue	Wed	Thu	Fri	Sat	Sun	Mon	Tue	Wed	Thu	Fri
44	FEB	1	2	3	4	5	6	7	8	9	10	11	12	13	14	15	16	17	18	19	20	21	22	23	24
45	momo01																								
46	momo02																								
47	momo03																								
48	momo04																								
49	momo05																								

Simultaneous update and display of changes

All staff can log in and edit the file at the same time

All updates and changes are shown simultaneously

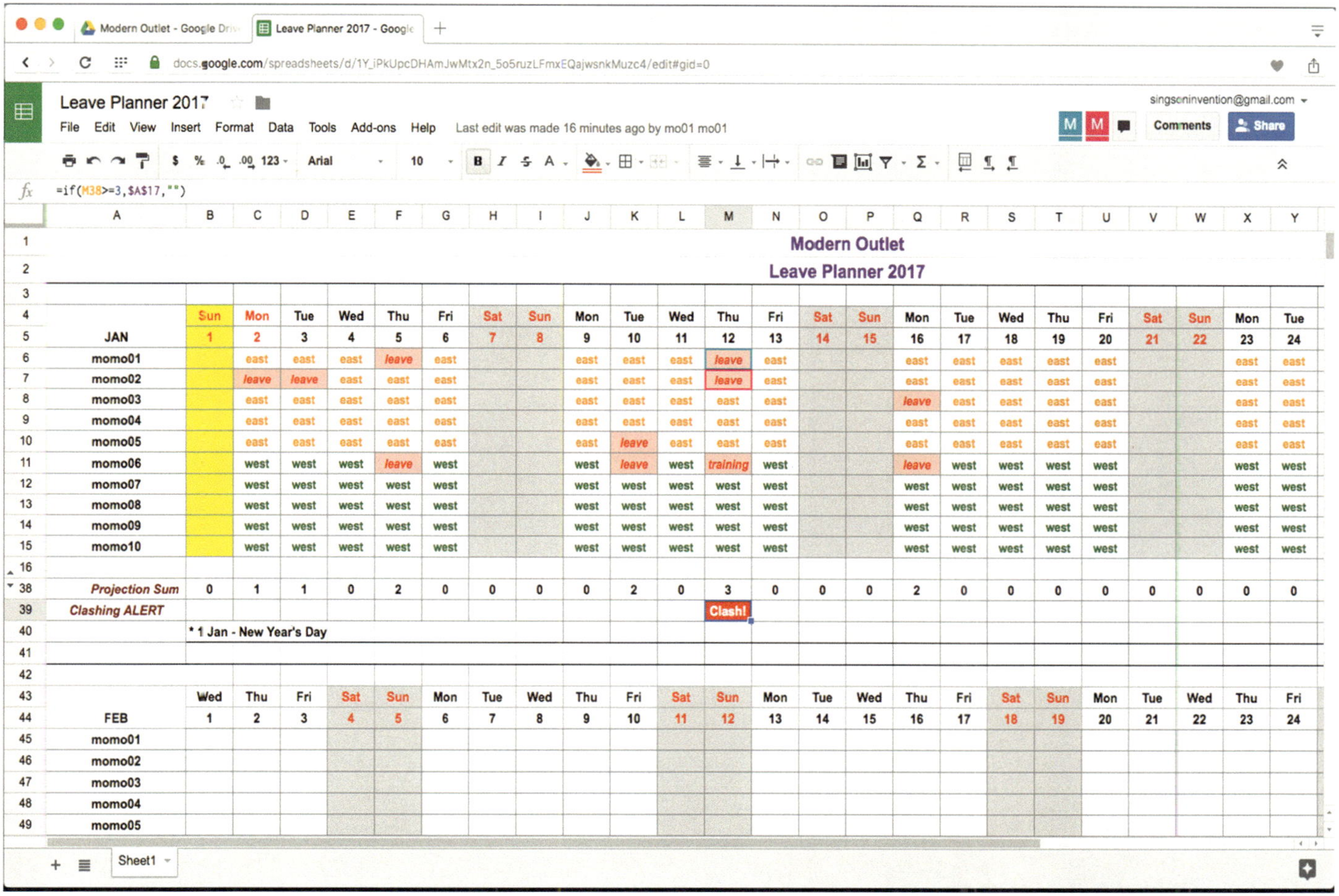
Modern Outlet - Google Drive | Leave Planner 2017 - Google

docs.google.com/spreadsheets/d/1Y_iPkUpcDHAmJwMtx2n_5o5ruzLFmxEQajwsnkMuzc4/edit#gid=0

Leave Planner 2017

File Edit View Insert Format Data Tools Add-ons Help Last edit was made 16 minutes ago by mo01 mo01

singsoninvention@gmail.com

Comments Share

fx =if(M38>=3,A17,"")

Modern Outlet

Leave Planner 2017

	A	B	C	D	E	F	G	H	I	J	K	L	M	N	O	P	Q	R	S	T	U	V	W	X	Y
4		Sun	Mon	Tue	Wed	Thu	Fri	Sat	Sun	Mon	Tue	Wed	Thu	Fri	Sat	Sun	Mon	Tue	Wed	Thu	Fri	Sat	Sun	Mon	Tue
5	JAN	1	2	3	4	5	6	7	8	9	10	11	12	13	14	15	16	17	18	19	20	21	22	23	24
6	momo01		east	east	east	leave	east			east	east	east	leave	east			east	east	east	east	east			east	east
7	momo02		leave	leave	east	east	east			east	east	east	leave	east			east	east	east	east	east			east	east
8	momo03		east	east	east	east	east			east	east	east	east	east			leave	east	east	east	east			east	east
9	momo04		east	east	east	east	east			east	east	east	east	east			east	east	east	east	east			east	east
10	momo05		east	east	east	east	east			east	leave	east	east	east			east	east	east	east	east			east	east
11	momo06		west	west	west	leave	west			west	leave	west	training	west			leave	west	west	west	west			west	west
12	momo07		west	west	west	west	west			west	west	west	west	west			west	west	west	west	west			west	west
13	momo08		west	west	west	west	west			west	west	west	west	west			west	west	west	west	west			west	west
14	momo09		west	west	west	west	west			west	west	west	west	west			west	west	west	west	west			west	west
15	momo10		west	west	west	west	west			west	west	west	west	west			west	west	west	west	west			west	west
16																									
38	*Projection Sum*	0	1	1	0	2	0	0	0	0	2	0	3	0	0	0	2	0	0	0	0	0	0	0	0
39	*Clashing ALERT*												Clash!												
40		* 1 Jan - New Year's Day																							
41																									
42																									
43		Wed	Thu	Fri	Sat	Sun	Mon	Tue	Wed	Thu	Fri	Sat	Sun	Mon	Tue	Wed	Thu	Fri	Sat	Sun	Mon	Tue	Wed	Thu	Fri
44	FEB	1	2	3	4	5	6	7	8	9	10	11	12	13	14	15	16	17	18	19	20	21	22	23	24
45	momo01																								
46	momo02																								
47	momo03																								
48	momo04																								
49	momo05																								

Sheet1

Clash alert is shown when there are more than 2 staff are indicated as absent from work – either “leave” or “training”

Staff momo06 has been arranged for training on 12-Jan

However, momo01 and momo02 project for leave on the same day

“Clash!” is shown in cell M39 to highlight the clashing

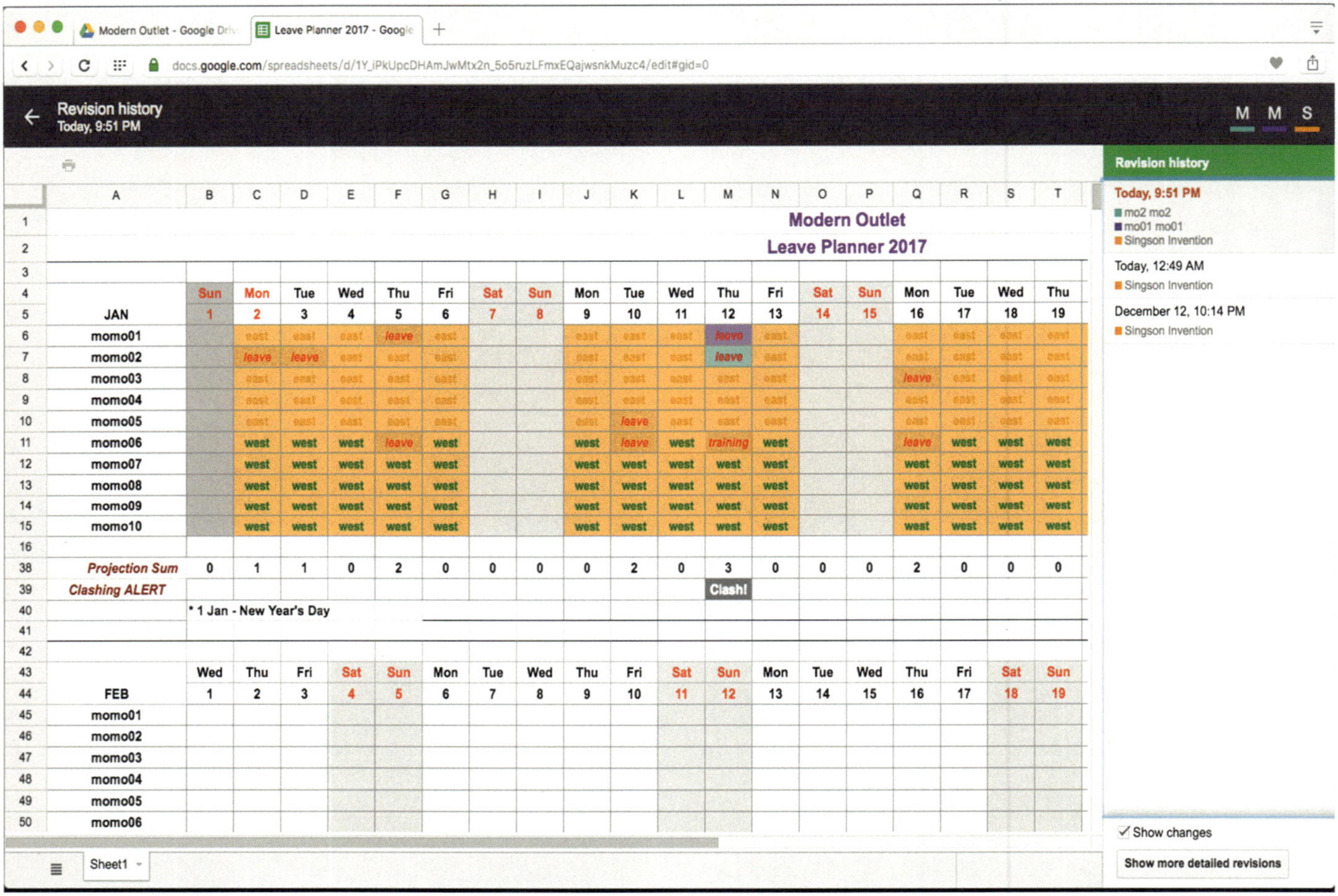

Tracking of revision history by the manager

Manager logs in as administrator to open the file → Go to toolbar → Left click "File" → Left click "See Revision History" → Press "Show more detailed revisions" in the right menu

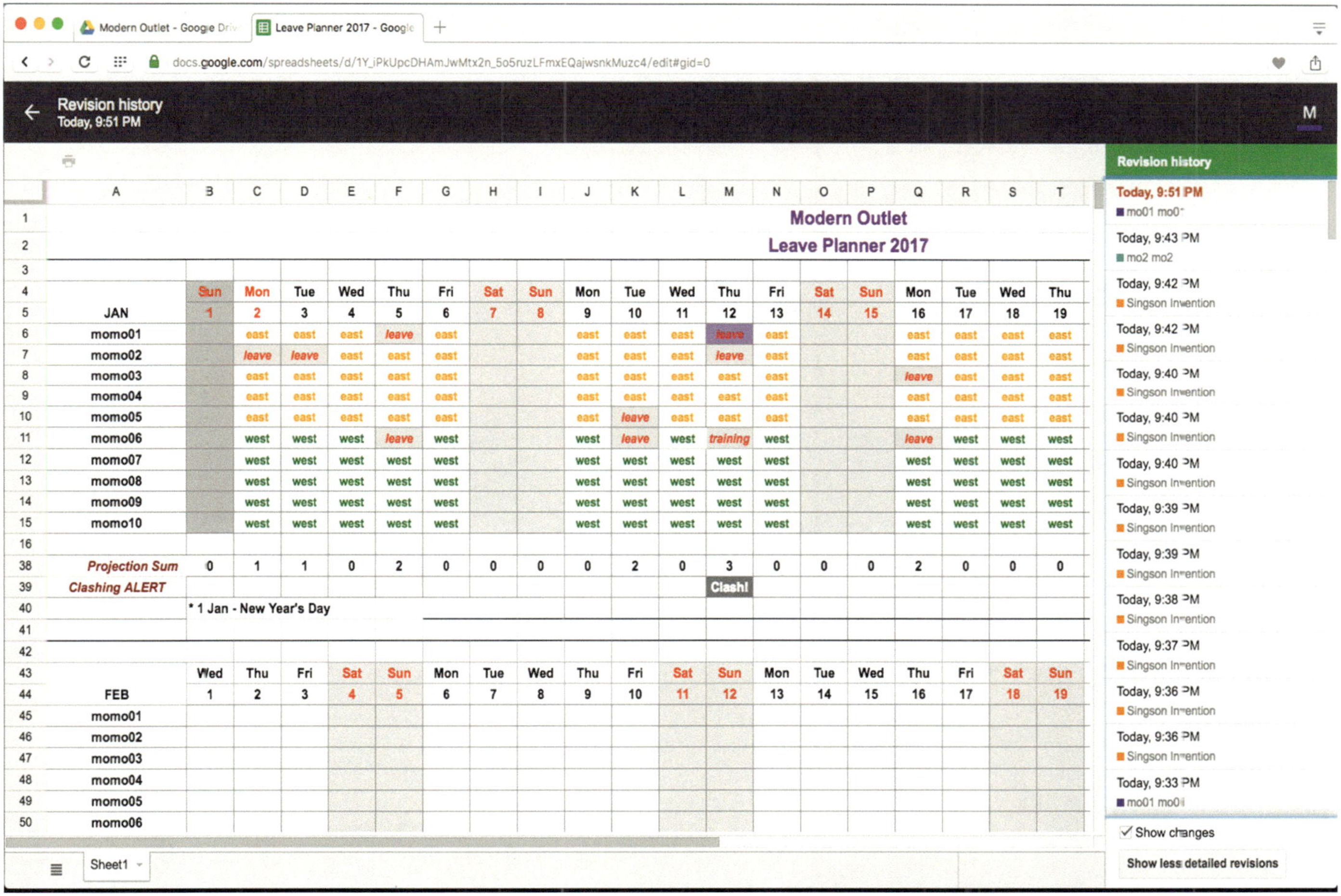

	A	B	C	D	E	F	G	H	I	J	K	L	M	N	O	P	Q	R	S	T
1													Modern Outlet							
2													Leave Planner 2017							
3																				
4		Sun	Mon	Tue	Wed	Thu	Fri	Sat	Sun	Mon	Tue	Wed	Thu	Fri	Sat	Sun	Mon	Tue	Wed	Thu
5	JAN	1	2	3	4	5	6	7	8	9	10	11	12	13	14	15	16	17	18	19
6	momo01		east	east	east	leave	east			east	east	east	leave	east			east	east	east	east
7	momo02		leave	leave	east	east	east			east	east	east	leave	east			east	east	east	east
8	momo03		east	east	east	east	east			east	east	east	east	east			leave	east	east	east
9	momo04		east	east	east	east	east			east	east	east	east	east			east	east	east	east
10	momo05		east	east	east	east	east			east	leave	east	east	east			east	east	east	east
11	momo06		west	west	west	leave	west			west	leave	west	training	west			leave	west	west	west
12	momo07		west	west	west	west	west			west	west	west	west	west			west	west	west	west
13	momo08		west	west	west	west	west			west	west	west	west	west			west	west	west	west
14	momo09		west	west	west	west	west			west	west	west	west	west			west	west	west	west
15	momo10		west	west	west	west	west			west	west	west	west	west			west	west	west	west
16																				
38	Projection Sum	0	1	1	0	2	0	0	0	0	2	0	3	0	0	0	2	0	0	0
39	Clashing ALERT												Clash!							
40		* 1 Jan - New Year's Day																		
41																				
42																				
43		Wed	Thu	Fri	Sat	Sun	Mon	Tue	Wed	Thu	Fri	Sat	Sun	Mon	Tue	Wed	Thu	Fri	Sat	Sun
44	FEB	1	2	3	4	5	6	7	8	9	10	11	12	13	14	15	16	17	18	19
45	momo01																			
46	momo02																			
47	momo03																			
48	momo04																			
49	momo05																			
50	momo06																			

Review the time sequence of the editing made by different staff

1. Left click the 1st row in the Revision history menu
2. The change(s) made by the staff will be highlighted in corresponding color
3. It is shown that momo01 projected his leave on 12-Jan at 9:51pm (cell M6 is in purple)

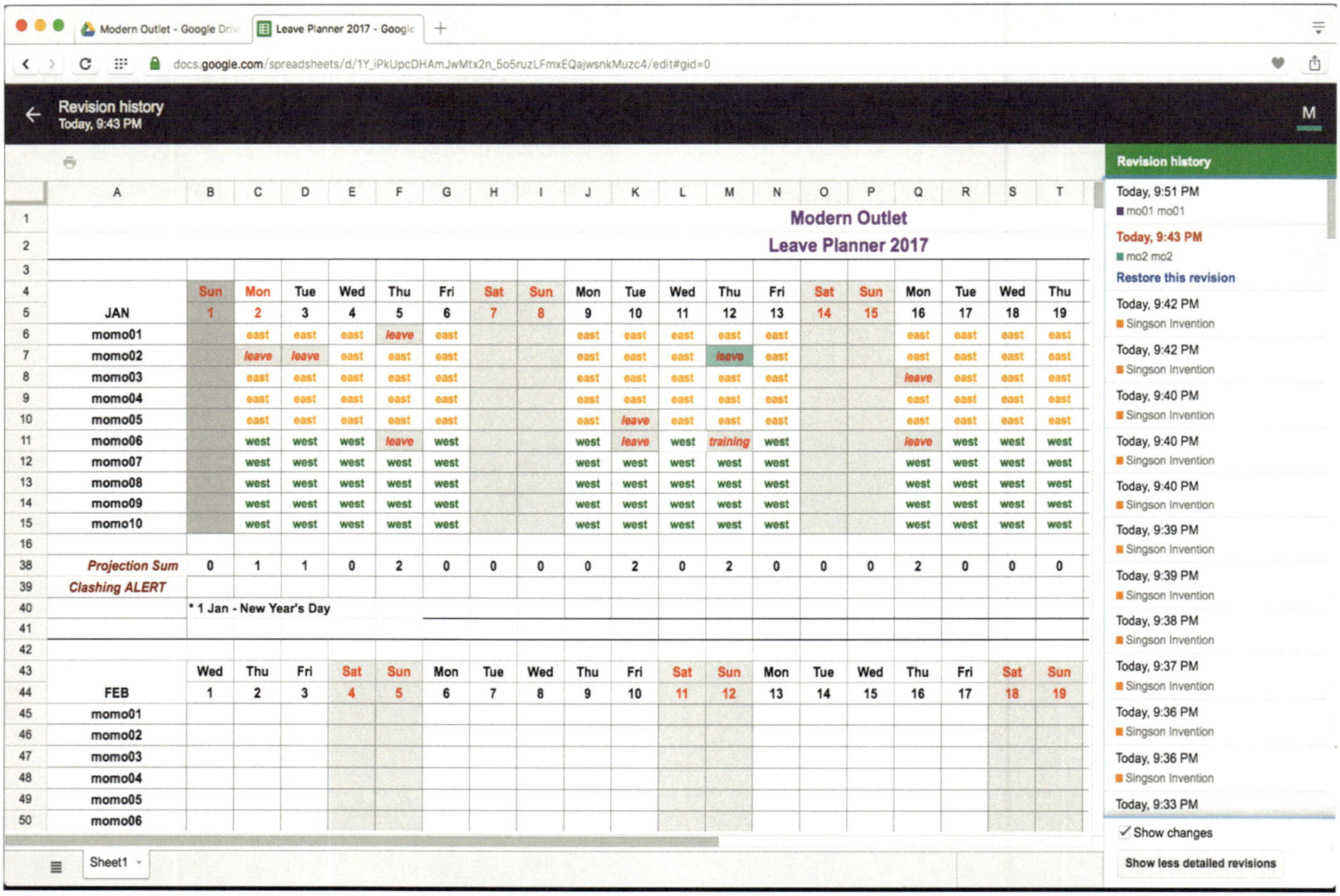

Review the time sequence of the editing made by different staff

Left click the 2nd row in the Revision history menu

It is shown that momo02 projected his leave on 12-Jan at 9:43pm (cell M7 is in green)

In other words, momo2 projected his leave earlier than momo01

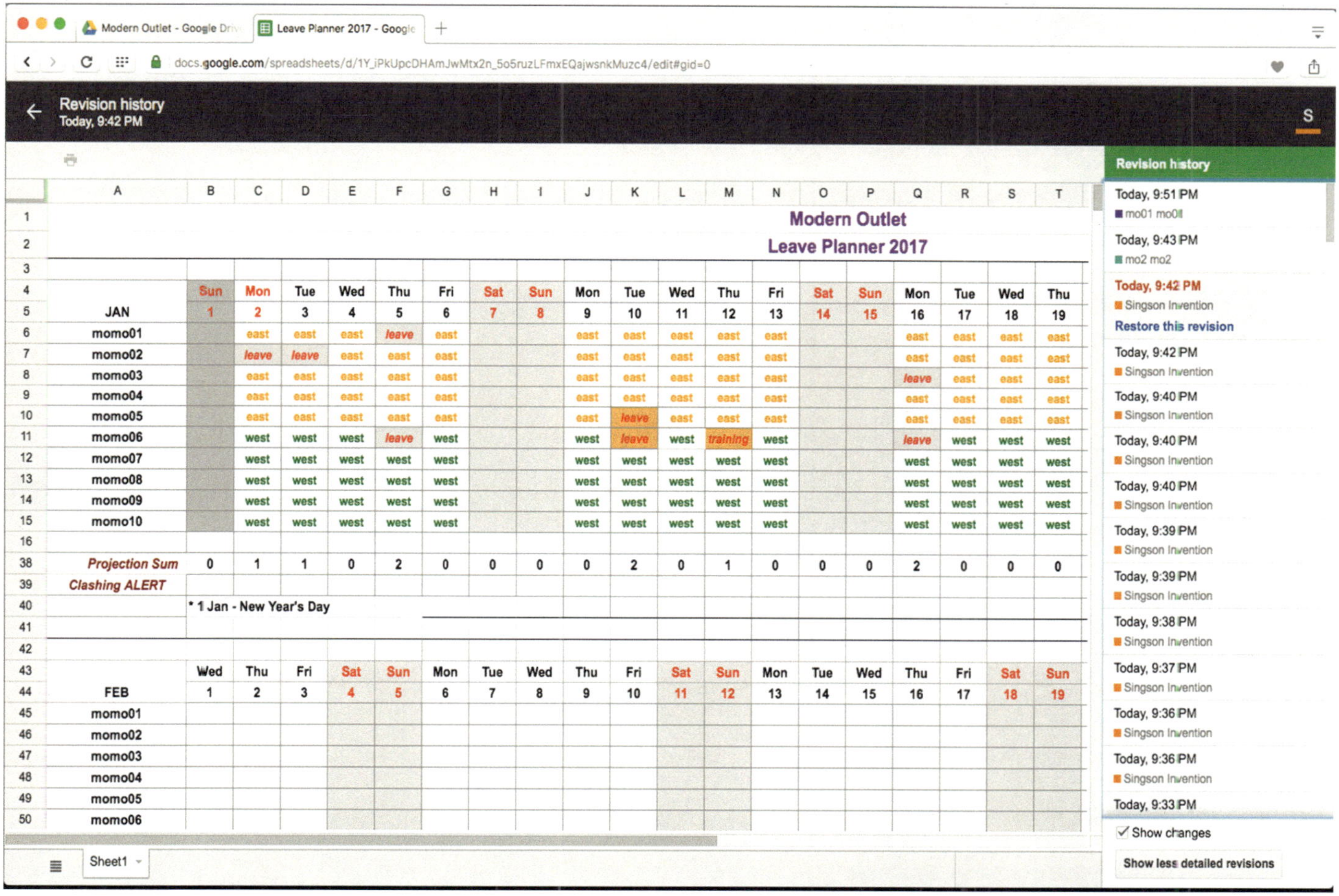

Review the time sequence of the editing made by different staff

Left click the 3rd row in the Revision history menu

It is shown that the manager arranged training for momo06 on 12-Jan at 9:42pm (cell M11 is in orange)

In other words, the manager has made training arranging for momo06 before leave projection by momo01 and momo02

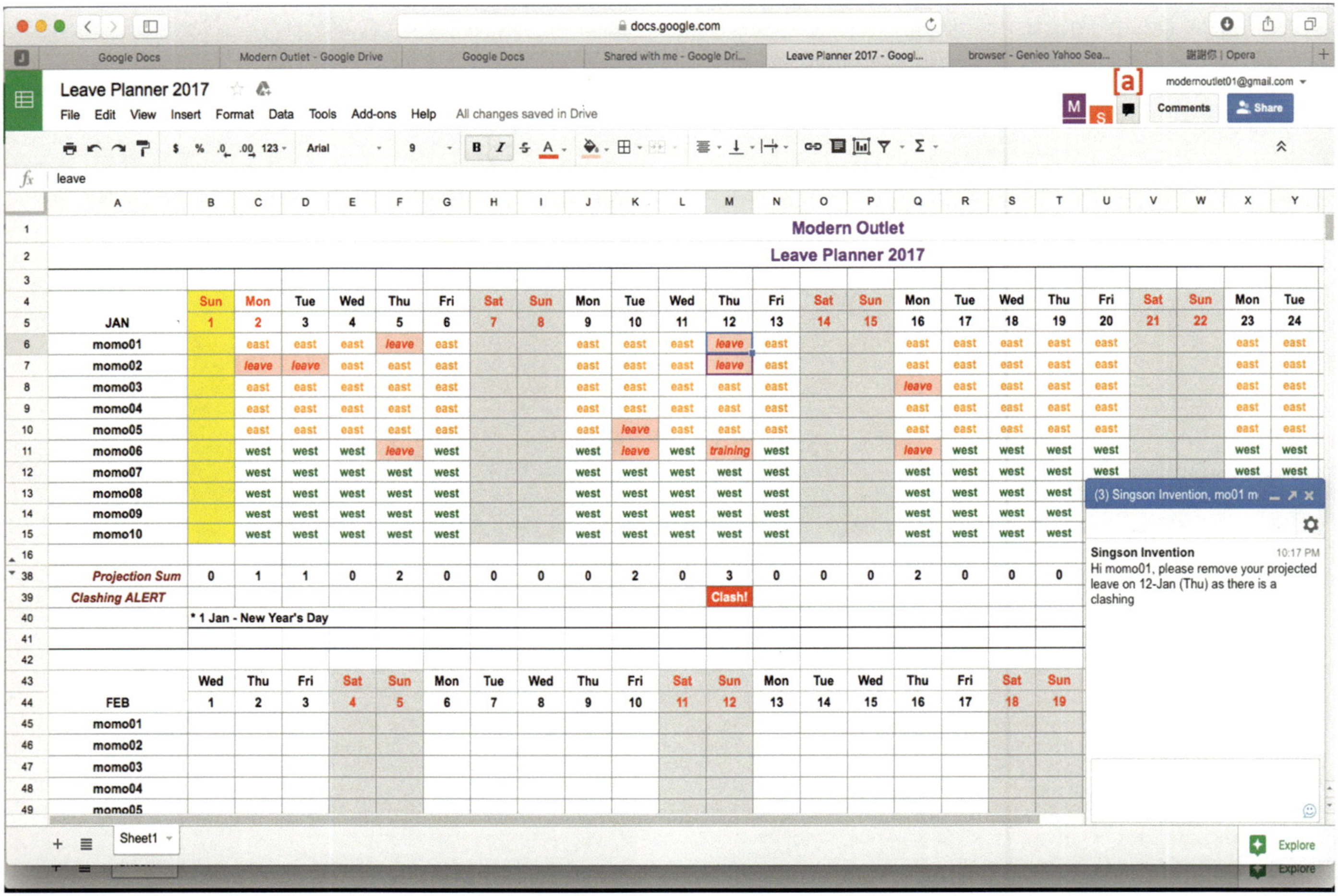

Manager notifies the staff momo01 to remove his leave by sending chat message

Left click the chat icon [a] → A chat window will be popped up → Type in the message in the chat window and press Enter

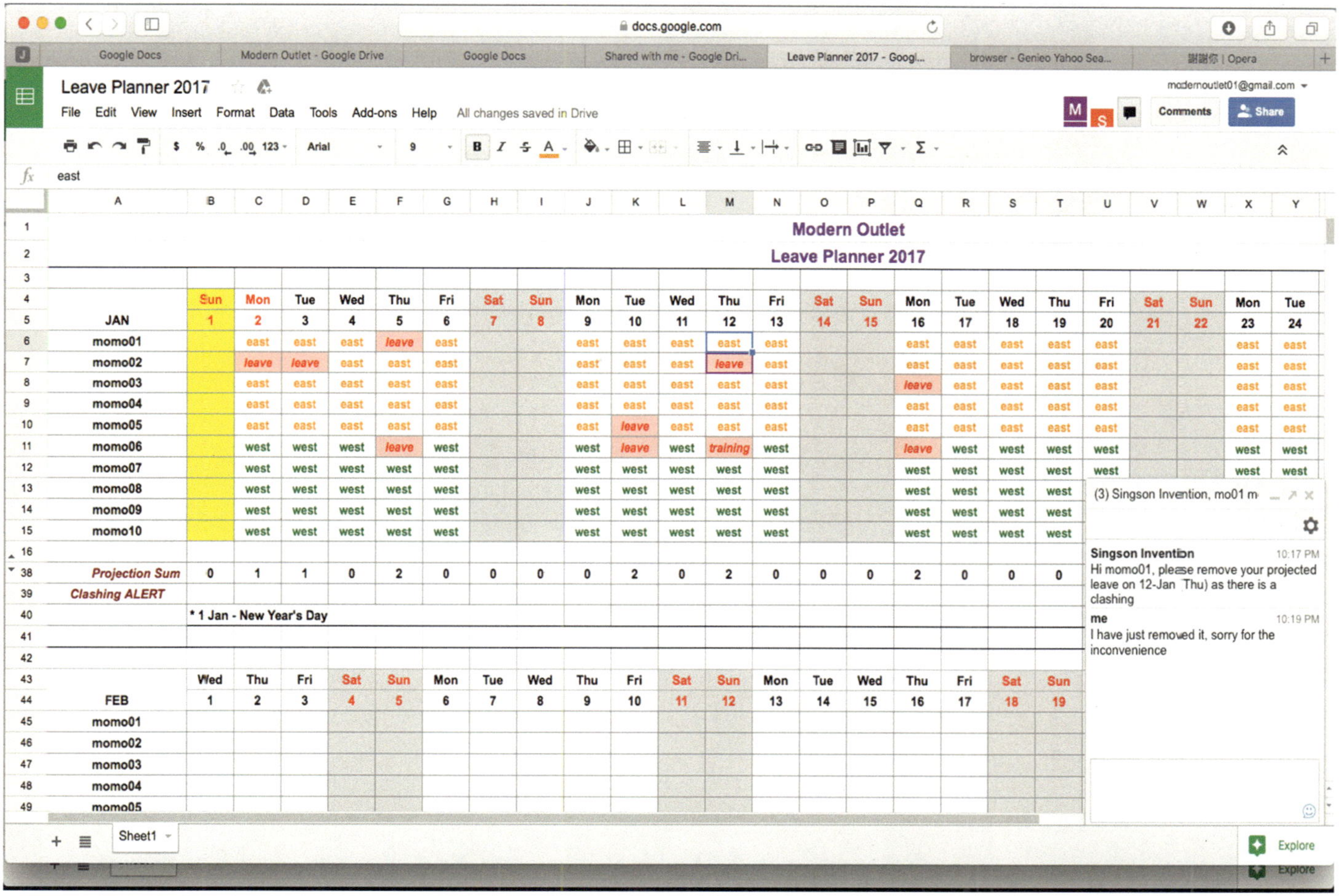

Staff momo01 views and replies the message sent by the manager

1. Staff momo01 logs in and open the file
2. Momo01 sees the message in the Chat window
3. Momo01 removes the leave on 12-Jan
4. Momo01 replies the manager change has been made

Chapter 7)

Lock the cells to disallow further changes made by staff

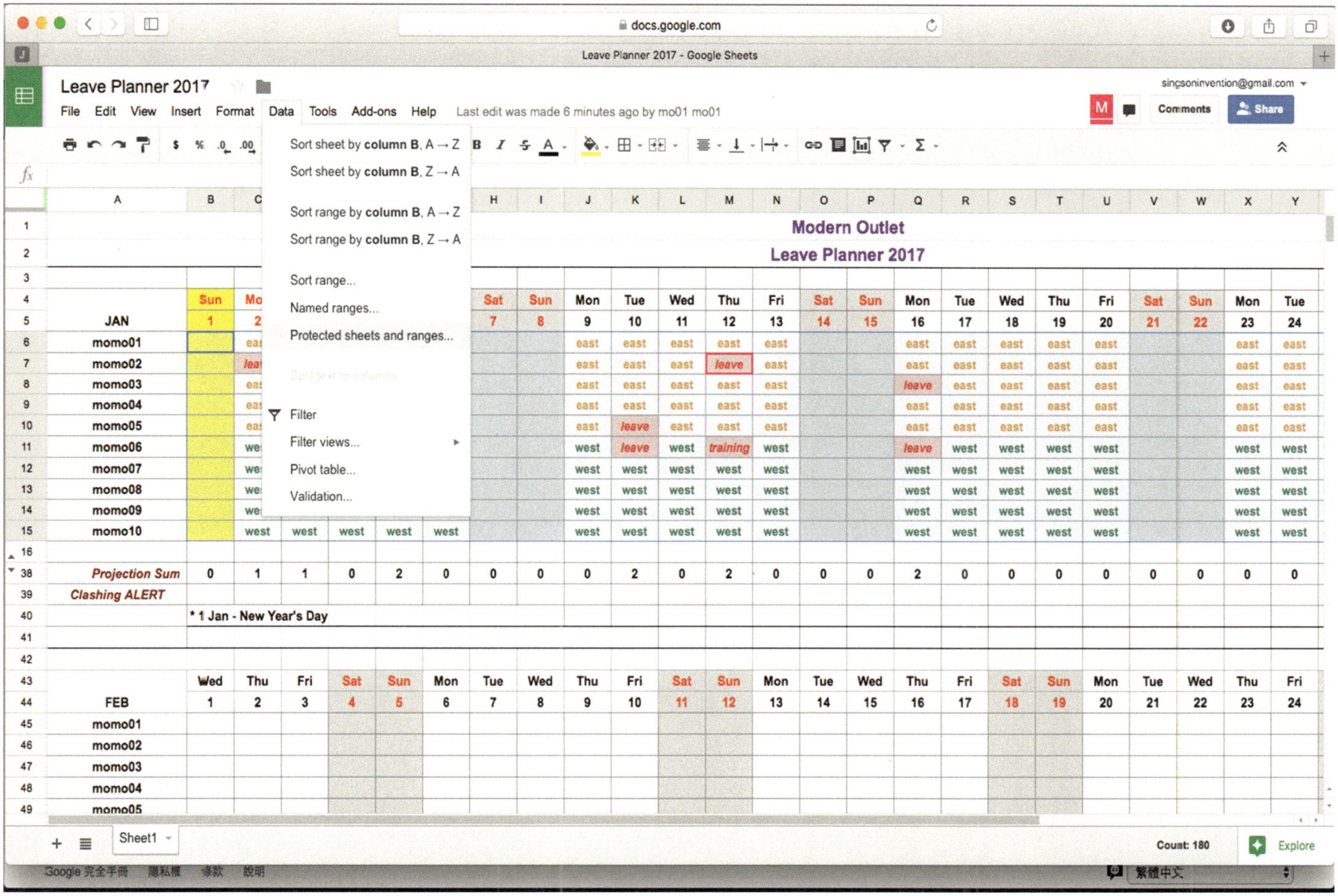

 # *After leave projection period is over, you want to disallow further changes by staff (e.g. 15-Jan is the last day for Feb leave projection)*

Remove editing permissions for all staff for all dates in Jan

1. Manager log in as administrator to open the file
2. Left click and hold to select row 6 to 15
3. Go to toolbar
4. Left click “Data”
5. Left click “Protected sheets and ranges”

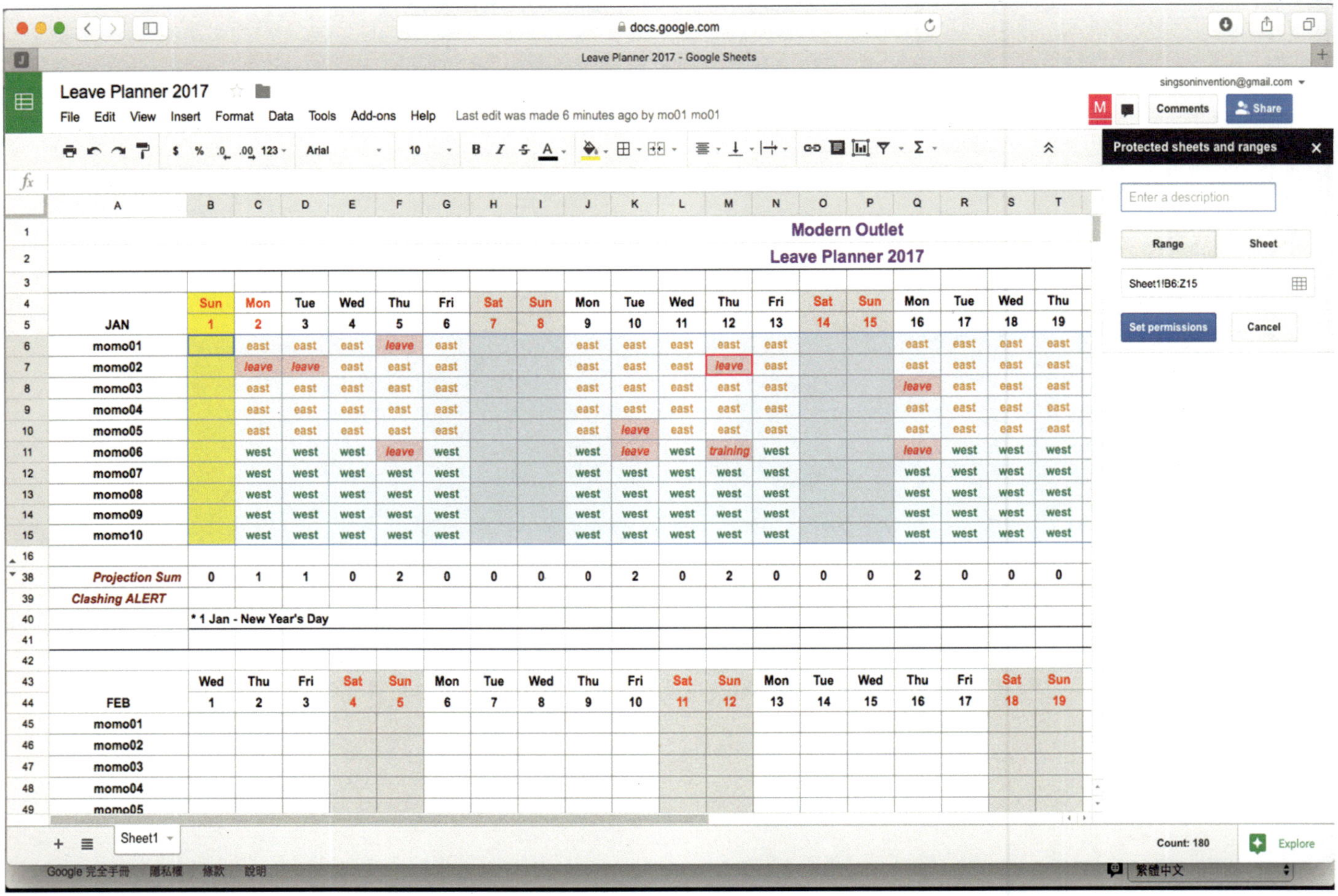

Remove editing permissions for all staff for all dates in Jan

Go to the right menu → Press "Set permissions"

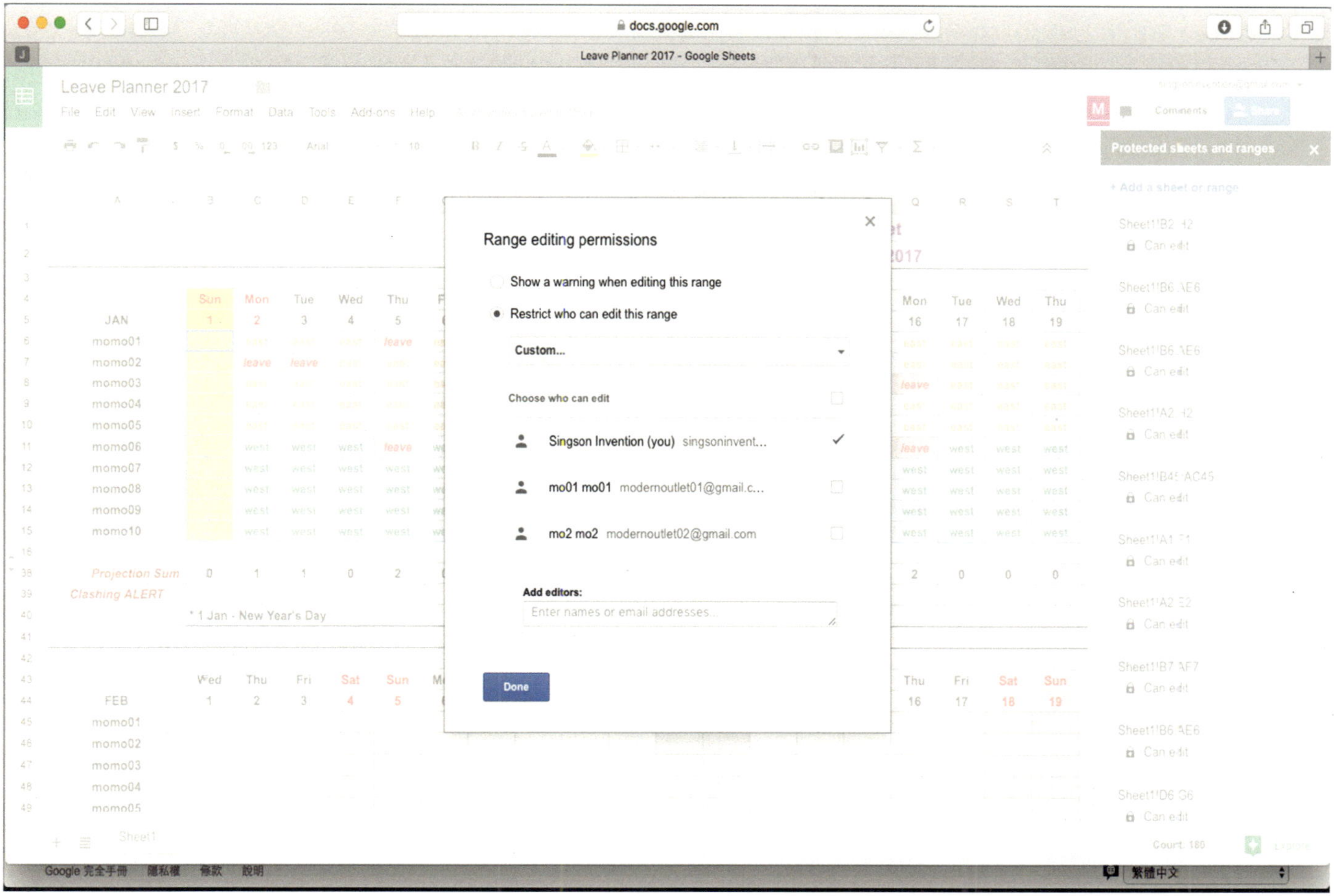

Remove editing permissions for all staff for all dates in Jan

1. Left click to "untick" the checked boxes for other staff
2. Press "Done" upon completion
3. Same setting can be done for the other months, when required

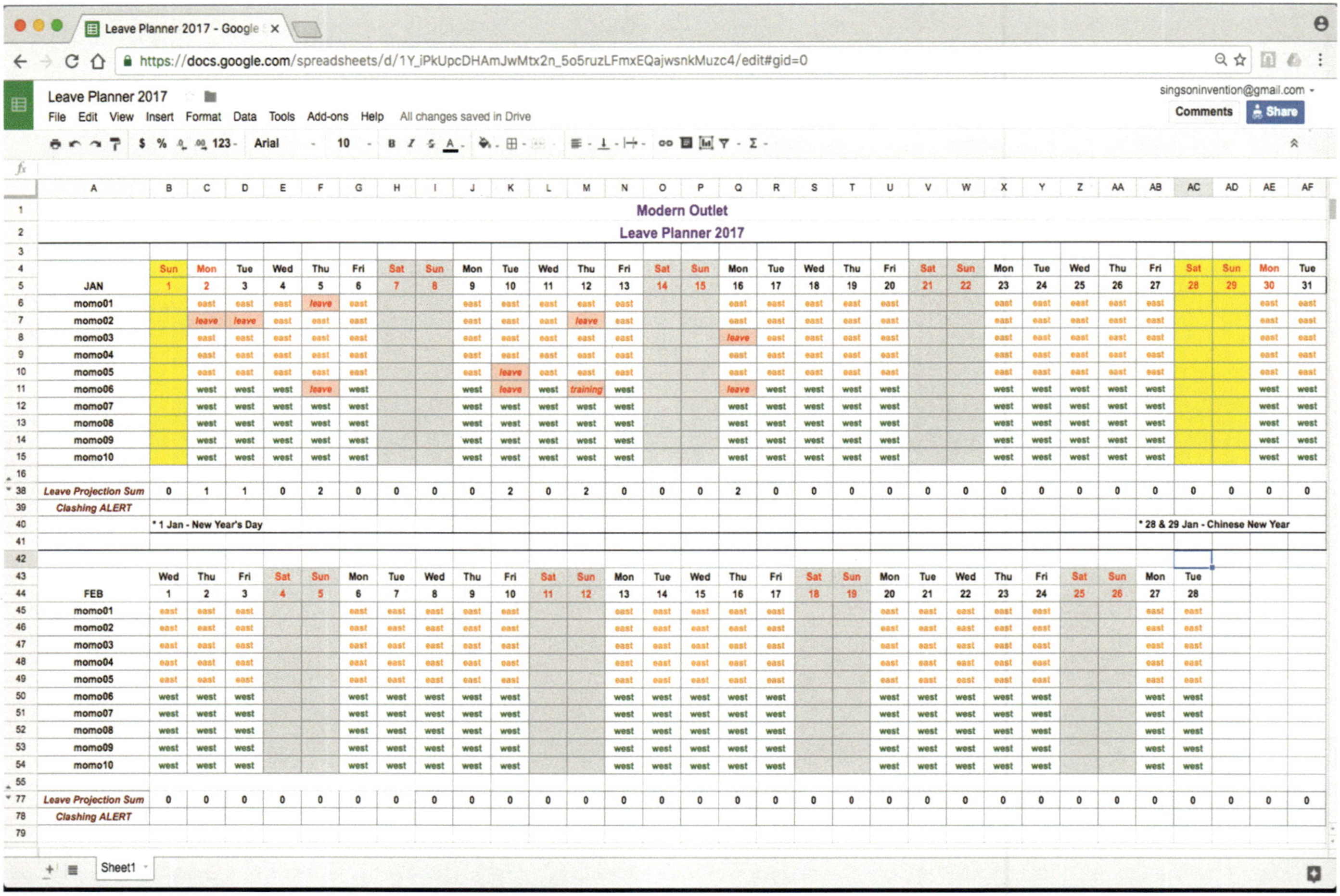

Modern Outlet

Leave Planner 2017

Row	A	B	C	D	E	F	G	H	I	J	K	L	M	N	O	P	Q	R	S	T	U	V	W	X	Y	Z	AA	AB	AC	AD	AE	AF
4		Sun	Mon	Tue	Wed	Thu	Fri	Sat	Sun	Mon	Tue	Wed	Thu	Fri	Sat	Sun	Mon	Tue	Wed	Thu	Fri	Sat	Sun	Mon	Tue	Wed	Thu	Fri	Sat	Sun	Mon	Tue
5	JAN	1	2	3	4	5	6	7	8	9	10	11	12	13	14	15	16	17	18	19	20	21	22	23	24	25	26	27	28	29	30	31
6	momo01		east	east	east	leave	east			east	east	east	east	east			east	east	east	east	east			east	east	east	east	east			east	east
7	momo02		leave	leave	east	east	east			east	east	east	leave	east			east	east	east	east	east			east	east	east	east	east			east	east
8	momo03		east	east	east	east	east			east	east	east	east	east			leave	east	east	east	east			east	east	east	east	east			east	east
9	momo04		east	east	east	east	east			east	east	east	east	east			east	east	east	east	east			east	east	east	east	east			east	east
10	momo05		east	east	east	east	east			east	leave	east	east	east			east	east	east	east	east			east	east	east	east	east			east	east
11	momo06		west	west	west	leave	west			west	leave	west	training	west			leave	west	west	west	west			west	west	west	west	west			west	west
12	momo07		west	west	west	west	west			west	west	west	west	west			west	west	west	west	west			west	west	west	west	west			west	west
13	momo08		west	west	west	west	west			west	west	west	west	west			west	west	west	west	west			west	west	west	west	west			west	west
14	momo09		west	west	west	west	west			west	west	west	west	west			west	west	west	west	west			west	west	west	west	west			west	west
15	momo10		west	west	west	west	west			west	west	west	west	west			west	west	west	west	west			west	west	west	west	west			west	west
16																																
38	Leave Projection Sum	0	1	1	0	2	0	0	0	0	2	0	2	0	0	0	2	0	0	0	0	0	0	0	0	0	0	0	0	0	0	0
39	Clashing ALERT																															
40		* 1 Jan - New Year's Day																										* 28 & 29 Jan - Chinese New Year				
43		Wed	Thu	Fri	Sat	Sun	Mon	Tue	Wed	Thu	Fri	Sat	Sun	Mon	Tue	Wed	Thu	Fri	Sat	Sun	Mon	Tue	Wed	Thu	Fri	Sat	Sun	Mon	Tue			
44	FEB	1	2	3	4	5	6	7	8	9	10	11	12	13	14	15	16	17	18	19	20	21	22	23	24	25	26	27	28			
45	momo01	east	east	east			east	east	east	east	east			east	east	east	east	east			east	east	east	east	east			east	east			
46	momo02	east	east	east			east	east	east	east	east			east	east	east	east	east			east	east	east	east	east			east	east			
47	momo03	east	east	east			east	east	east	east	east			east	east	east	east	east			east	east	east	east	east			east	east			
48	momo04	east	east	east			east	east	east	east	east			east	east	east	east	east			east	east	east	east	east			east	east			
49	momo05	east	east	east			east	east	east	east	east			east	east	east	east	east			east	east	east	east	east			east	east			
50	momo06	west	west	west			west	west	west	west	west			west	west	west	west	west			west	west	west	west	west			west	west			
51	momo07	west	west	west			west	west	west	west	west			west	west	west	west	west			west	west	west	west	west			west	west			
52	momo08	west	west	west			west	west	west	west	west			west	west	west	west	west			west	west	west	west	west			west	west			
53	momo09	west	west	west			west	west	west	west	west			west	west	west	west	west			west	west	west	west	west			west	west			
54	momo10	west	west	west			west	west	west	west	west			west	west	west	west	west			west	west	west	west	west			west	west			
55																																
77	Leave Projection Sum	0	0	0	0	0	0	0	0	0	0	0	0	0	0	0	0	0	0	0	0	0	0	0	0	0	0	0	0	0	0	0
78	Clashing ALERT																															

#You may set up a monthly leave projection timeline for your department using this planner as the platform. Below is an example.

Advance planning of staff training and staff self-projected leave

The manager may set a start and cut-off date for leave projection for the next month

E.g. Staff can start to project for Feb leave from 01 Jan onward and the cut-off date is on 15 Jan

After 15 Jan, all cells in Feb will be locked and no further changes can be made by staff

By 21 Jan, the roster and leave results for Feb will be finalized and released to all staff

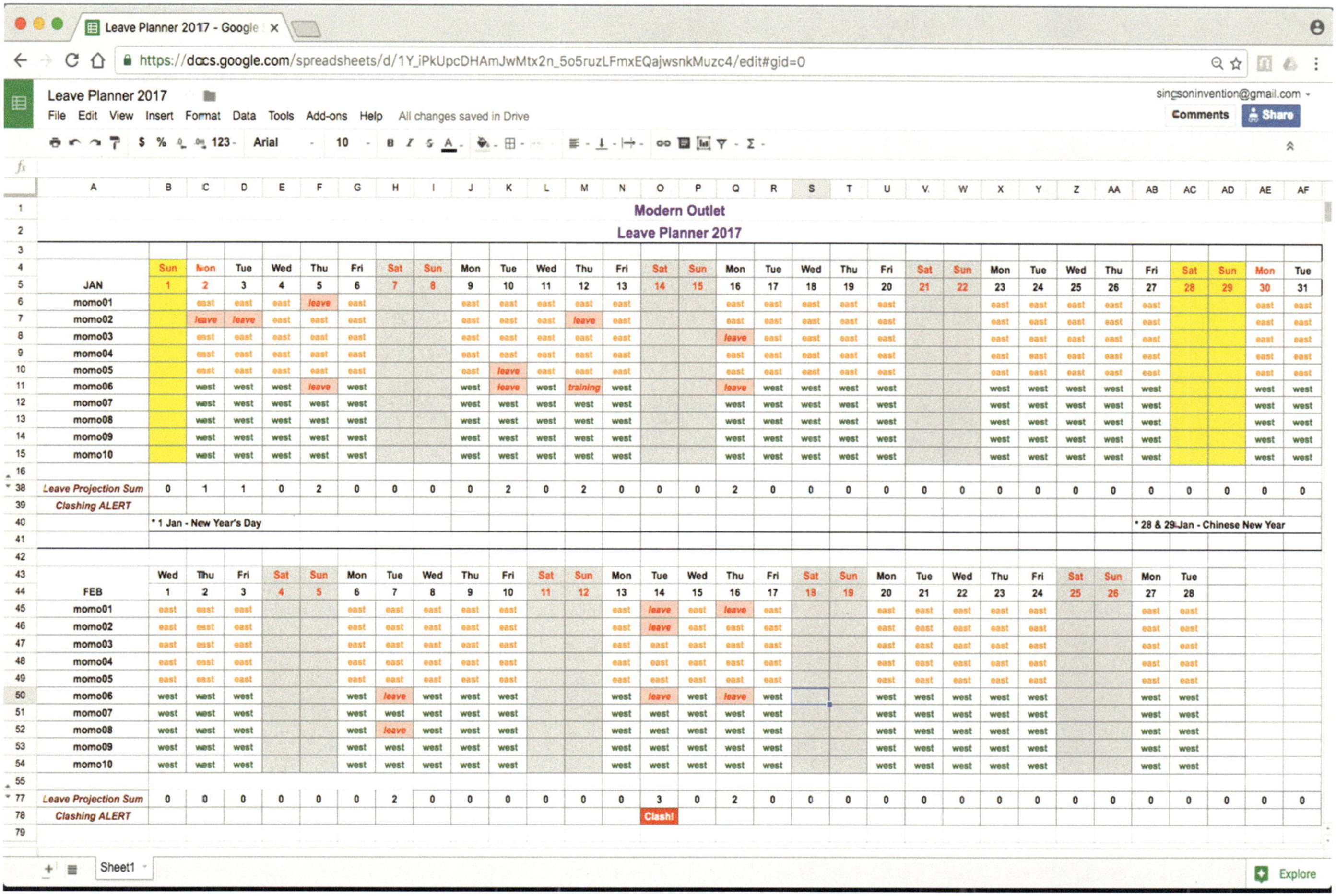

Modern Outlet

Leave Planner 2017

	Sun	Mon	Tue	Wed	Thu	Fri	Sat	Sun	Mon	Tue	Wed	Thu	Fri	Sat	Sun	Mon	Tue	Wed	Thu	Fri	Sat	Sun	Mon	Tue	Wed	Thu	Fri	Sat	Sun	Mon	Tue
JAN	1	2	3	4	5	6	7	8	9	10	11	12	13	14	15	16	17	18	19	20	21	22	23	24	25	26	27	28	29	30	31
momo01		east	east	east	leave	east			east	east	east	east	east			east	east	east	east	east			east	east	east	east	east			east	east
momo02		leave	leave	east	east	east			east	east	east	leave	east			east	east	east	east	east			east	east	east	east	east			east	east
momo03		east	east	east	east	east			east	east	east	east	east			leave	east	east	east	east			east	east	east	east	east			east	east
momo04		east	east	east	east	east			east	east	east	east	east			east	east	east	east	east			east	east	east	east	east			east	east
momo05		east	east	east	east	east			east	leave	east	east	east			east	east	east	east	east			east	east	east	east	east			east	east
momo06		west	west	west	leave	west			west	leave	west	training	west			leave	west	west	west	west			west	west	west	west	west			west	west
momo07		west	west	west	west	west			west	west	west	west	west			west	west	west	west	west			west	west	west	west	west			west	west
momo08		west	west	west	west	west			west	west	west	west	west			west	west	west	west	west			west	west	west	west	west			west	west
momo09		west	west	west	west	west			west	west	west	west	west			west	west	west	west	west			west	west	west	west	west			west	west
momo10		west	west	west	west	west			west	west	west	west	west			west	west	west	west	west			west	west	west	west	west			west	west
Leave Projection Sum	0	1	1	0	2	0	0	0	0	2	0	2	0	0	0	2	0	0	0	0	0	0	0	0	0	0	0	0	0	0	0
Clashing ALERT																															
	* 1 Jan - New Year's Day																										* 28 & 29 Jan - Chinese New Year				

	Wed	Thu	Fri	Sat	Sun	Mon	Tue	Wed	Thu	Fri	Sat	Sun	Mon	Tue	Wed	Thu	Fri	Sat	Sun	Mon	Tue	Wed	Thu	Fri	Sat	Sun	Mon	Tue			
FEB	1	2	3	4	5	6	7	8	9	10	11	12	13	14	15	16	17	18	19	20	21	22	23	24	25	26	27	28			
momo01	east	east	east			east	east	east	east	east			east	leave	east	leave	east			east	east	east	east	east			east	east			
momo02	east	east	east			east	east	east	east	east			east	leave	east	east	east			east	east	east	east	east			east	east			
momo03	east	east	east			east	east	east	east	east			east	east	east	east	east			east	east	east	east	east			east	east			
momo04	east	east	east			east	east	east	east	east			east	east	east	east	east			east	east	east	east	east			east	east			
momo05	east	east	east			east	east	east	east	east			east	east	east	east	east			east	east	east	east	east			east	east			
momo06	west	west	west			west	leave	west	west	west			west	leave	west	leave	west			west	west	west	west	west			west	west			
momo07	west	west	west			west	west	west	west	west			west	west	west	west	west			west	west	west	west	west			west	west			
momo08	west	west	west			west	leave	west	west	west			west	west	west	west	west			west	west	west	west	west			west	west			
momo09	west	west	west			west	west	west	west	west			west	west	west	west	west			west	west	west	west	west			west	west			
momo10	west	west	west			west	west	west	west	west			west	west	west	west	west			west	west	west	west	west			west	west			
Leave Projection Sum	0	0	0	0	0	0	2	0	0	0	0	0	0	3	0	2	0	0	0	0	0	0	0	0	0	0	0	0	0	0	0
Clashing ALERT														Clash!																	

Example of Jan & Feb roster, training and leave planner

All staff can project their Feb leave from 01 to 15 Jan

Manager will lock all the cells for Feb on 16 Jan

Manager will communicate to staff for Clash! (eg 14-Feb); Manager then makes changes if needed

By 21 Jan, the roster and leave results for Feb will be finalized and released to all staff

Troubleshooting & FAQ

Chapter 1) – Create shared folder and Sheets file:

1) Can the staff provides you with non-Gmail email account?

Ans/Possible causes: If the staff email is a non-Gmail address, he can only view the Sheets file through the hyperlink that you have sent him through invitation. However, he will not be allowed to perform any editing.

Suggested solutions: Please advise the staff to provide a usable Gmail account or to apply for one if he does not possess one, so as to enable the editing function of the planner for leave projection. (should there be a requirement).

Chapter 2) – Set up conditional formatting rules:

1) If the reasons (i.e. wordings) for absent from work are more than “leave” and “training”, what should I do?

Ans/Possible causes: You can tailor the leave planner according to your department needs, this includes adding in other “official” reasons of absence in conditional formatting.

Suggested solutions: You can add in additional criteria during conditional formatting setting. For example, create additional rule for text contains “meeting” in addition to “leave” and “training”. You may refer to Chp.2 – “Set up Conditional Formatting Rules” for details. One thing to take note is you will need to create additional cells and rows for “Auto-counting” function to count the number of “meeting” for all staff. For example, replace the word “leave” with “meeting” in the sample formula **=IF(ISNUMBER(SEARCH(“leave”, B6)),1,0)** and makes it become **=IF(ISNUMBER(SEARCH(“meeting”, B6)),1,0)**. After that, include all the cells in “Projection Sum” calculation together with Auto-counting rows for “Leave” and “Training” so that all 3 criteria are taken into account for Clash Alert identification. Please refer to Chp.3 – Set up clashing alert using tailor-made formulas” for details.

Chapter 3) – Set up clashing alert using tailor-made formulas:

1) If the number of staff that is allowed to be absent from work is different on different dates and different months, can it be done?

Ans/Possible causes: In cells and rows that tie to Clash Alert setting, you can amend the formula according to your need.

Suggested solutions: Amend the formula, replace the "=>3" with another number in the sample formula, for example, in cell B39 **=IF(B38=>3,A17,"")**, change the "=>3" to "=>1"and convert it into **=IF(B38=>1,A17,"")** if you only allow 1 staff member to be absent on that date instead of 2 staff members due to peak season demand.

Chapter 5) – Set up staff-specific editing permissions for cells and rows

1) After setting permissions to a specific staff member, why are other staff members allowed to edit those cells as well?

Ans/Possible causes: When setting permissions, you can only select cells in the SAME row and apply the setting to the cells of the same row. If you select cells for multiple rows at the same time, for example select B6 to AF6 in Jan for staff momo01 (same row), then keep pressing "Contrl" to select B45 to AF45 in Feb for staff momo01 (another row) and then apply permission setting, the setting may not work to its desired effect.

Suggested solutions: Only apply permissions setting to the cells in the SAME row. Set up for one row for one staff at a time and avoid multiple rows selection.

Chapter 5) – Set up staff-specific editing permissions for cells and rows

2) One staff reflects that he cannot edit the cells that he has been given permissions to (e.g. staff momo01 can only view, but unable to edit the cells B6 to AF6 in Jan).

Ans/Possible causes: After assigning permissions of certain cells to a staff, the permissions of those cells should not be changed and reassigned to another staff (e.g. initially permissions assigned wrongly to staff momo02, but then the permissions were in turn, being reassigned to momo01). Otherwise, the latter mom02, who was later assigned with the permissions may not be able to edit the cells.

Suggested solutions: Do not reassign the permissions to another staff. You can insert another row below, then copy the contents of the previous row and paste it to the newly inserted row. Then apply new permissions setting to the new row to the appropriate staff. Once done, delete the row that is wrongly set previously. One thing to take note is you will need to check the formula settings in cells that are involved in calculation of "clashing alert " and edit the formulas of the affected cells due to the relative cells shifting after row insertion and deletion. If you have difficulty in editing the formulas of those cells, the simplest way is to re-do the clashing alert setting for that particular month. Please refer to the starting page of Chp. 3 – "Set up clashing alert using tailor-made formulas" for details.

Other general questions

1) Can the non- team members or 'outsiders' view the Sheets file?

Ans/Possible causes: You have the discretion in deciding on whosoever you deem to have the privilege of viewership of the files. whether staff members or otherwise.

Suggested solutions: You can change the setting in "Share with others" (Right click the Sheets file and left click "Share..."). Choose either "Anyone with the link can view" to "OFF – only specific people can access" based on your actual need and preference.

2) Why the Sheets file cannot be accessed or opened?

Ans/Possible causes: You may not be able to access or open the file when there are problems or glitches associated with the internet network or Google Server conditions. Other likely causes could be that your account had suffered sustained malicious attacks by unknown parties. That may trigger Google to auto-freeze your account due to security considerations.

Suggested solutions: Try to log in and open the file past hoc. If your account is frozen by Google due to security reasons, reset the password following Google's instructions. Consider employing more sophisticated password and change your password regularly to minimize the chance of being hacked. It will be good to have a regular "static" back up of your Sheets file in case of retrieval failure. This can be done by copying the contents of the Sheets file and paste them to a blank MS Excel file in a regular schedule. You can do it at the end of every week or every month, remember to date the file and save it to a folder in your computer drive (local drive or external drive).

Made in the USA
Las Vegas, NV
09 November 2026

57764358R00040